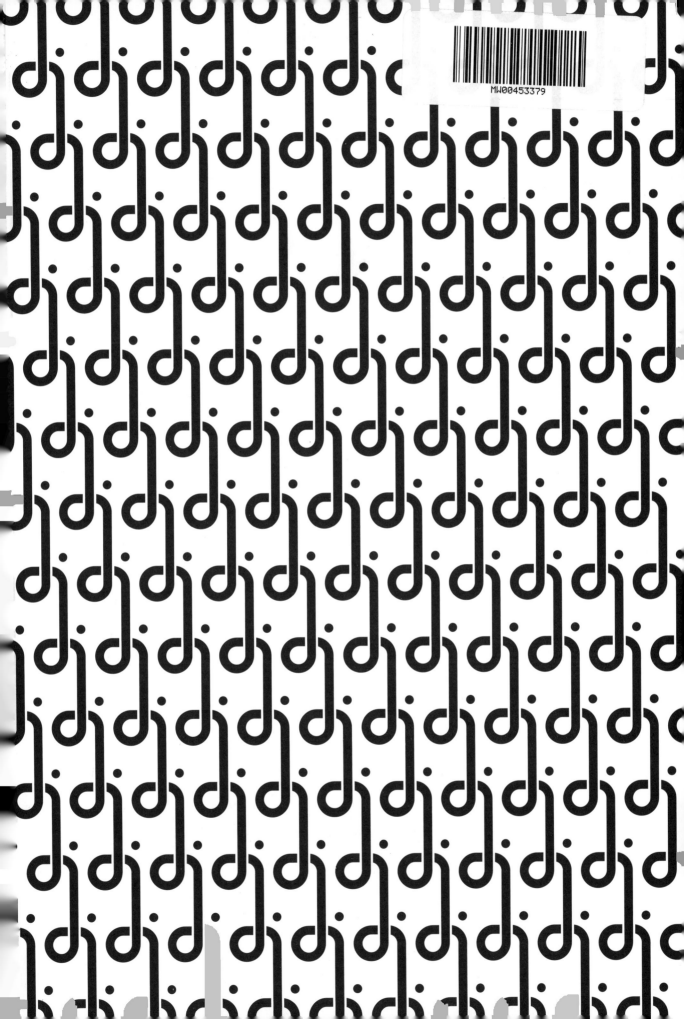

MW00453379

BIS Publishers
Borneostraat 80 A
1094 CP Amsterdam
The Netherlands
T + 31 (0)20 515 02 30
bis@bispublishers.com
www.bispublishers.com

ISBN 978 90 6369 603 0

Every reasonable attempt has been made to identify owners of copyright.
Any errors or omissions brought to the publisher's attention will be corrected in subsequent
editions.

Editing: Allison Hiew
Layout, styling & production: Tanya Desplat
Full-colour illustrations: Joshua Neale at Love Letters Studio
www.lovelettersde.com (CC BY-ND 4.0)
Di logo & tool templates: Erez Nusem
Sketches & timeline: Karla Straker

DESIGN INNOVATION

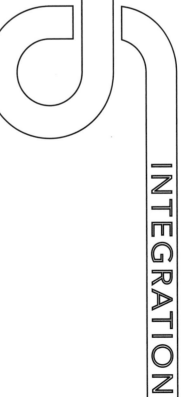

INTEGRATION

STRAKER, WRIGLEY & NUSEM

CONTENTS

6   DEDICATION
7   THE AUTHORS
8   FOREWORD
10   KEY TERMS
12   INTRODUCTION
14   THIS BOOK
16   BOOK MANUAL
18   THE BASICS
22   A SHORT EVOLUTION OF THE THEORIES OF
       Design Thinking, Design Innovation & Design Integration
30   200 YEARS OF DESIGN & INNOVATION TIMELINE
36   DESIGN TOOLS

42   DESIGN INNOVATION
43   The Components

48   CONSIDER
52   Core Stakeholders
54   Stakeholder Map
58   Organisational Conditions Framework
60   Driving Questions Consider

64   AUDIT
68   Core Insight
72   Business Model Analysis
78   Customer Segment Profile
80   Driving Questions Audit

84   INTENT
88   Core Value
90   Value Definition
94   Design Brief
98   Driving Questions Intent

102   DESIGN
106   Core Skills
110   Design Philosophy & Practice
114   Design Critique & Criteria
116   Driving Questions Design

120   IMPLEMENT
124   Core Communication
126   Pitching
130   Business Case
134   Driving Questions Implement

138   EVALUATE
142   Core Metrics
144   Driving Questions Evaluate
146   SUMMARY

DESIGN INTEGRATION   **150**

DESIGN CATALYST   **154**
Capabilities of the Design Catalyst   154
Designer Intuition   154
Business Acumen   155
Agile Facilitation   156
Customer Centred   157
Rule Breaker   157
Research Rigour   158
Value of the Design Catalyst   159
TAKEAWAYS   159

ORGANISATIONAL CONDITIONS   **166**
Strategic Vision   166
Facilities   168
Cultural Capital   169
Directive(s)   169
TAKEAWAYS   172
Organisational Conditions Audit   174
Organisational Conditions Matrix   176

THINKING STYLES   **180**
Systems Thinking   181
Design Thinking   182
Creative Thinking   182
Thinking Approaches   184
Integrated Thinking   186
TAKEAWAYS   187

DESIGN PRINCIPLES   **190**
Sucky Semantics   191
No Culture   191
Solutioneering   192
Feeling isolated   192
Disconnected?   193
Stifled creativity   193
Driven by metrics   194
Scared to fail   194
Struggling to commit   195
TAKEAWAYS   195

CONCLUSION   **196**
TOOL TEMPLATES   **200**
REFERENCES   **234**

DEDICATION

We dedicate this book to **Dr Judy Matthews** for her constant wisdom and support. Few people are as giving with their time and expert opinion. We have traveled the world together on a quest to push the boundaries of design (back before it was popular) and into the unknown. Without your support, the three of us would not be where we are today!
Thank you Judy

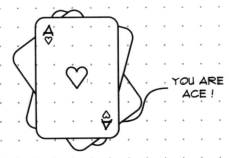

YOU ARE ACE !

THE AUTHORS

CARA WRIGLEY, PHD

KARLA STRAKER, PHD

EREZ NUSEM, PHD

Dr Straker, Professor Wrigley and **Dr Nusem** are proud Queenslanders, colleagues, friends and at one stage even roommates. We have travelled the world together and fought over cereal, task timelines, and what colour the cover of this book should be. We have thrived together as a team and now after a decade of tormenting each other we practically speak our own design language – we would not have it any other way. Being proud Australians means we don't take life too seriously (nor ourselves for that matter); we get to do what we love and love what we do.

Our day jobs consist of running the **Design Innovation Research Group**, (hosting industry research projects from a range of sectors), a university-wide Design Major (teaching design to hundreds of undergrads), and a Master's Program on Design Innovation and Strategic Design at the University of Sydney (where did we find the time to write this book, we hear you ask!) We are educators, innovators, and above all designers! We are not afraid to get things wrong and celebrate our successes along with our failures. We work with numerous multi-disciplinary teams and collaborate on large research projects in the Sydney Nano Institute, Sydney's Westmead Hospital, and the Innovative Cardiovascular Engineering and Technology Laboratory (ICETLAB) at the Prince Charles Hospital in Brisbane.

We have kept busy in the last decade working with businesses from a plethora of industries to explore a design approach to innovation – this includes start-ups and global organisations in both the private and public sectors. To name a few, we have formed partnerships with TAFE NSW, BiVACOR, WaterCo, Suncorp Insurance, Commonwealth Bank of Australia, Enmodes GmbH and the Royal Australian Airforce. We have published in the most prestigious business and design periodicals – Berkeley's California Management Review, Strategy & Leadership and, the MIT Press, Design Issues. This will be our third book together and (probably) not our last. We have inspired international audiences through countless conferences, won global and national awards for our work, and had a fun time doing it!

We have learnt that finding people you not only enjoy working with but who challenge you is rare. Finding people who you trust and become your family after a decade is even rarer – so cheers to us and doing the near impossible every day.

FORE
WORD

The discipline of design has historically been defined as the process of planning and creating ideas, and implementing these ideas to improve the artificial and natural environment. Our landscape is constantly changing - whether due to technology trends and advancements, customer demands or global competition. Of course, adapting to these changes requires new approaches and disciplines to emerge. This book presents our current knowledge surrounding design's value to business, which has been shaped by our engagements with industry and the research discoveries of recent decades. It outlines the new thinking required in a design process to address current and future challenges, highlighting adaptations that have occurred over the years and challenging the current design thinking process.

Design thinking has been adopted as a tool for innovation in a range of organisations in a broad range of industries. One common misconception is that design can be treated as a checklist (where the practitioner works through a series tools in a structured process), this will not lead to innovative outcomes or strategic change within an organisation. There is a need for more explicit guidance in the form of learning resources, as well as approaches that support organisations in applying and implementing design innovation. This book therefore provides theoretical and practical understandings of design innovation and integration to add to the growing number of design resources.

Little is known about the lasting effects of design thinking inside organisations. This is largely because the current focus remains on the principles, practices and methods rather than its longevity. Part 1 of this book provides an easily accessible overview of the design innovation process, along with a specialised selection of methods and tools that can be applied across different contexts. To us, **design innovation** is the examination and creation of novel solutions – this could include a product, service, business model or any other output emerging from design. Design innovation as a process considers the:

✕ organisation
✕ customer
✕ wider social and industry context.

This process is supported by a set of tools, and this book provides activities to help the reader better understand the purpose and underlying theory for each of these tools. We don't just cover how to use the tools, but also *why* the tools should be used in the first place. The book is designed as a learning resource, with the first chapters scaffolding the reader's understanding of the theory and evolution of design innovation and integration. Each component of a design innovation process is then detailed, along with some examples of corresponding tools. Each tool is explained with:

✗   a small theoretical background
✗   its placement in the overall process
✗   step-by-step instructions for use.

Ready-to-use templates for reproduction under the creative commons licence can be found at the back of this book for most tools discussed (plus some extras).

Design integration (Part 2) is the long-term adoption of design innovation within an organisation. This part of the book introduces the reader to the principles and practices of design, design catalysts, thinking styles, innovation types and the organisational conditions required for design. With this knowledge, the reader can strategically lead and apply design in a workplace. Design leaders seeking to undertake design integration within their organisations are provided with a process to follow, and with tips to overcome the potential challenges they might face. Different thinking styles are examined to demonstrate outcomes from varying approaches to innovation and how they can be applied to elevate an organisation's competitive position. The organisational conditions required for design integration are detailed, allowing the reader to identify design's relationship to the strategic aspects of an organisation. Part 2 is written to serve as a reference for design leaders seeking to integrate design into their business practices and to create a conducive environment for design. This part of the book is unique in providing insights on implementing design innovation within organisations.

The methods outlined in this book have been created, tested and iterated over the past 10 years in collaborations with industry and higher education programs across the disciplines of design, business, engineering, arts, social science, law, medicine and science. This book is written by qualified designers for non-designers, providing customised templates to guide the practical application of design through a collection of tools and methods.

STRAKER, WRIGLEY & NUSEM

Our other books:

Wrigley, C. & Straker, K. (2018), **Affected: Emotionally Engaging customers in the Digital Age**, Wiley.
Nusem, E., Wrigley, C. & Straker, K. (2020), **Design Innovation for Health and Medicine**, Palgrave McMillian.

Like to work with us? Get in contact

🐦 @di_syd
(or google our names for our lastest contact details)

KEY TERMS

- ✗ **AUDIT (COMPONENT):** a set of activities undertaken by a designer to acquire insights that will inform the design

- ✗ **ASSUMPTION:** an opinion that is believed to be true, but has not been confirmed through evidence

- ✗ **BUSINESS MODEL:** how an organisation creates and captures value

- ✗ **COMPETITIVE ADVANTAGE:** the factors or attributes that allow an organisation to exceed its mpetitors

- ✗ **CONSIDER (COMPONENT):** preliminary efforts made by a designer to understand and unpack the context for design

- ✗ **CUSTOMER:** a person who purchases goods or service (not necessarily a user)

- ✗ **CUSTOMER INSIGHT:** an interpretation of a customer's latent needs and feelings gathered through design methods

- ✗ **DESIGN:** the process of planning, creating ideas, and implementing these ideas to improve the artificial and natural environment

- ✗ **DESIGN CATALYST CAPABILITIES:** a set of six essential skills required by a DC for the implementation of design innovation

- ✗ **DESIGN CATALYST:** a designer who leads design thinking interventions within an organisation

- ✗ **DESIGN CATALYST (DC):** the person responsible for doing and driving a design inside an organisation

- ✗ **DESIGN CHAMPION:** a person with a senior position in an organisation that sponsors design activity

- ✗ **DESIGN INNOVATION:** the process of examining and creating novel solutions and outputs

- ✗ **DESIGN INNOVATION PRINCIPLE:** a guiding instruction or rule that drives the design process

- ✗ **DESIGN INTEGRATION:** the top-down and bottom-up approach to disseminating and adopting design inside an organisation

- ✗ **DESIGN INTERVENTION:** any form of design activity or engagement within a firm (e.g., a project, workshop, or design sprint)

- ✗ **DESIGN PHILOSOPHY:** your understanding of design knowledge which helps to guide your design practice and principles

- ✗ **DESIGN PRACTICE:** your own approach to designing, should continue to develop with experience

- ✗ **DESIGN PRINCIPLES:** a set of rules that align with your design philosophy and guide your design practice

- ✗ **DESIGN SKILLS:** the fundamental competency and expertise required to design

- ✗ **DESIGN STRATEGY:** the nexus between corporate strategy and design thinking

- ✗ **DESIGN TEAMS:** a group of creative thinkers and doers involved in a design project

- ✗ **DESIGN THINKING:** a cognitive process in which design concepts are developed

- ✗ **ETHNOGRAPHY:** the study of people in their natural habitat

✗ EVALUATE (COMPONENT): the process of assessing if a design has been successful and whether the designer's intent has been achieved

✗ IDEATION: the process of generating thoughts, ideas, or concepts

✗ IMPLEMENT (COMPONENT): the practice of translating an idea or concept into something real and tangible (e.g. a launched product or service)

✗ INSIGHT: novel data about a customer or business that can be used to create an innovative design

✗ INTENT (COMPONENT): a component of design that assists the designer to frame what value they are seeking to create and for whom

✗ KEY PERFORMANCE INDICATOR (KPI): is a measurable value that is used to show if a target has been met efficiently and effectually by an employee inside a business

✗ METHOD: a research procedure or protocol

✗ METRICS: a measurement that can be used to assess a design against a range of criteria

✗ NEW PRODUCT DEVELOPMENT (NPD): an industry term explaining the process a company goes through to develop a new product to make it into the market

✗ OFFERING: also referenced sometimes as 'value' – an outcome produced that may contribute to a stakeholder's life

✗ ORGANISATIONAL CONDITIONS: the internal factors that influence the uptake of design and how much support design is given in a business

✗ OUTCOME: how something turns out or occurs as a consequence

✗ OUTPUTS: the thing (e.g. product, service, business model, etc.) produced through the design process

✗ POST-IT NOTES: an expensive but useful piece of paper which has become a symbol of design and a central part of a novice- or non-designer's arsenal

✗ PRODUCT: a tangible thing or artefact that is produced through design

✗ SERVICE: the design of an operation and experience to meet customer or business objectives

✗ STAKEHOLDER: the parties that influence or are influenced by a design outcome or output

✗ TEMPLATE: a starting point, which usually consist of prompting questions and steps – always aim to make your own which accurately represent your project requirements (many included in the back of this book)

✗ THINKING STYLES: how an individual prefers to use their cognitive abilities to represent and process information, rather than the actual contents of their thinking process

✗ TOOL: a suggestion on a process to gain information usually supported by a template

✗ USER: the person that will use the output of design (not necessarily a customer)

✗ VALUE: something of importance or worth

✗ VALUE PROPOSITION: the core benefit(s) a company provides to a customer or stakeholder

INTRODUCTION

FIFTEEN YEARS AGO, COMPANIES COMPETED ON PRICE. TODAY IT'S QUALITY. TOMORROW IT'S DESIGN.

— **Robert Hayes, Harvard University (1991)**

TOMORROW IS TODAY!

Design and innovation are two words that have had a monumental increase in the realm of business in the past decade. A quick scroll through profiles on LinkedIn would reveal a multitude of job titles (either self-created or company-directed) comprised of the keywords design, innovation, and user-centred. This is quite a contrast to when we first started researching design's value in business in 2010: there was very little interest or activity to be seen.

Yet interest in design did begin to grow, with calls for research from a variety of fields (e.g., marketing, business management, strategy and information systems) to advance design theory and methods in business practice. This interest also extends to popular press articles published in Harvard Business Review, Forbes, Bloomberg Businessweek, The Economist, and Fast Company. There is a clear desire to understand this area more deeply — particularly how this knowledge can be translated into practical outcomes for companies.

We have been researching and developing our own method to integrate design within organisations (from the very small to the very, very, very large). Through our experience, we have always believed that design is more than the use of a collection of tools (especially the misconception that using post-it notes means you are designing) or following a step-by-step process (design is not a checklist that you follow to achieve success). Good design is never the result of a particular tool or moving through a number of methods — as these will never be created for your exact context of use. Rittel and Webber (1973) explain that throughout the process of designing, the designer is presented with many choices that guide the form of the final solution. Invariably, these choices are also framed by the constraints presented within a project (Rittel & Webber, 1973). Being a good designer is about understanding why you should use a particular tool, the shortcoming of the methods at your disposal, and knowing when you need to change or modify the process to suit your particular context. Therefore, we believe that you must first explore, debate, and leverage a strong theoretical understanding of design actions and skills before conceiving a process of your own.

The role of design has changed over the years, with terms like design thinking becoming increasingly popular. One distinction made between design and design thinking is that design thinking encompasses the cognitive processes that designers use, rather than the designed objects they create (Dunne, Martin & Rotman, 2006). This illustrates how design is evolving beyond its traditional boundaries in graphic, product, and interaction domain knowledge, into a method for solving complex problems. Today's complex or 'wicked problems' (Buchanan, 1992)[1] are often referenced as the reason for design's rapid up-take in non-design contexts. Designers – through their ability to conduct analysis that combines empathy, creativity, and rationality to provide solutions – are well equipped to manage such problems. This has been further reinforced by: the success of design in many leading organisations such as Apple, Coca-Cola and Deloitte; its link to innovation in executive and management practices; and its support from notable institutions (e.g., IDEO and the Stanford D-School), where design thinking is conceptualised as a way for non-designers to evaluate and use design methods.

[1] Wicked problems can be defined by lacking immediate solutions, are requiring the management of many stakeholders with conflicting priorities.

THIS BOOK

Thinking is required to get the most out of this book. Don't take us at our word, question our assumptions and yours (as anyone can call themselves a designer, and everyone calls themselves an expert). Other books will provide you a step-by-step process, methods that eliminate uncertainty and procedures that are 'no-brainers' for guaranteed success – all while promising improvement without risk. With such approaches the process does the work; the person implementing the process doesn't need to think. It's a process that leaves you feeling good, throwing your hands up to the design gods while screaming hallelujah!

But, with any design innovation and integration approach, the people executing the method, project, or organisational change are critical. Methods will aid you, but they won't be able to ever replace the innovator – who is, in a way, the artist. Methods can only enable the innovator. They are a tool, like a hammer for a carpenter, or CAD (computer-aided design software that helps with designing and drafting a building) in the hands of an Architect. These tools enable the abilities of the protagonist, but the skills of a master are still required to do the work.

All successful designers have their unique design processes – think of Frank Gehry (he is an architect, for those playing at home). His unique style was a product of his unique design process[2]. You must first create, test and understand your own unique design process. By all means, start with a step-by-step process, but don't stop there! Make it unique to you; to the project requirements, and to the organisation you are in. Ensure that after each experience you reflect and amend your process to understand what worked and what didn't. We don't follow a step-by-step process when we design, no matter the project size, scope, or requirements. We create one.

TOOLS ENABLE SKILLS.
YOU MUST HAVE THESE
SKILLS FIRST.

[2] Gehry is known for drawing spontaneous, bold sketches that inform his designs' sculptural forms

WE HAVE INCLUDED SOME ACTIVITIES IN THE DESIGN COMPONENT AND 'MUST KNOW DESIGNS' ON THE TIMELINE TO HELP YOU OUT.

The methods in this book are not a guarantee. In the hands of unmotivated people, these methods will yield no benefit. Design is a process of hard work, many unknowns, and creativity. Design innovation considers people, the design of outputs and the business environment. It requires thinking about products and services that strategically support the business – and a business that supports its people.

In this book, we present the six key components of design innovation, along with six corresponding core aspects that articulate the focus of each component. The practice of implementing different components changes when the situation requires it, so remember that no two projects are the same. The tools provided should be considered as a starting point. Not an exhaustive or prescribed approach, but rather a springboard for you to create your own tools and approaches.

The templates included at the back of this book are there to assist you in this journey. We have found them useful in our projects. This might not be the case for you, and you may have to (in fact we encourage you) pull them apart, change key questions, cross-out sections or completely re-design them for your own purpose.

We have provided examples of how the tools have been used to assist in the 'how to' side of things. Even if you don't fill them out or complete them as prescribed, they will aid in the facilitation of a conversation with team members or project stakeholders. This is the beauty of such tools and templates: understanding what it helps you think about or facilitate is often more important than completing them. After you have redesigned them or reinvented them for your own projects, we would love to know about it, so please get in contact (we will geek out on it, really). Throughout the book, you will find some notes with key reminders or questions to muse over, along with bulleted takeaways. We have also left room for you to write your own notes or visualise any thoughts you have along the way – we believe it's a great way to reflect on and implement what you've learnt.

NO APPROACH IS APPROPRIATE TO EVERY BRIEF, AND ONE BOOT CAMP DOES NOT MAKE A DESIGNER!

THERE ARE MANY WAYS TO DESIGN AN OUTCOME. IT'S UP TO YOU TO FIRST UNDERSTAND YOUR OBJECTIVES, AND THEN CREATE YOUR OWN APPROACH.

BOOK MANUAL

START AT THE BEGINNING OR THE END OR EVEN IN THE MIDDLE.
NO ANSWERS- JUST MORE QUESTIONS.
DOCUMENT EVERYTHING!

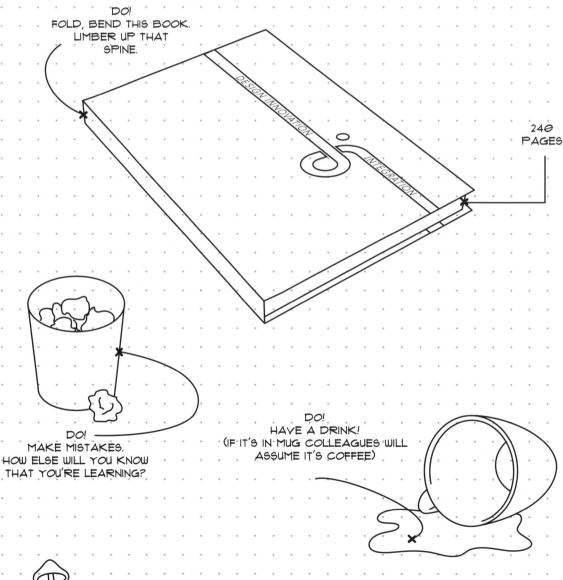

DO!
FOLD, BEND THIS BOOK.
LIMBER UP THAT
SPINE.

DESIGN INNOVATION
INTEGRATION

240
PAGES

DO!
MAKE MISTAKES.
HOW ELSE WILL YOU KNOW
THAT YOU'RE LEARNING?

DO!
HAVE A DRINK!
(IF IT'S IN MUG COLLEAGUES WILL
ASSUME IT'S COFFEE)

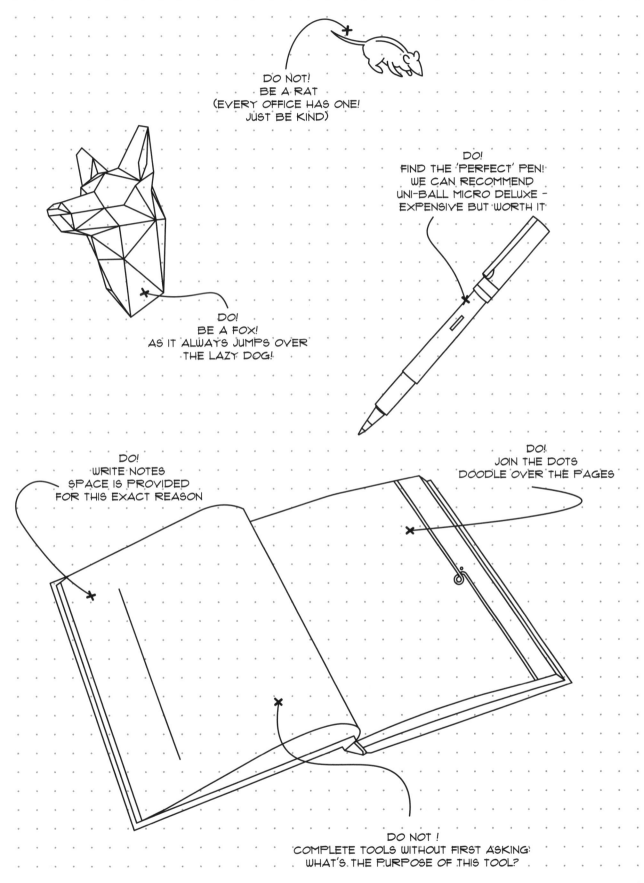

THE BASICS

THE BUSINESS OF DESIGN

Design can bring a range of commercial benefits if used appropriately across an organisation. The effective use of design gives customers a reason to buy from you and not from your competitors. It's a valuable source of differentiation, as a well-designed product or service will stand out from the competition. However, design can also provide value beyond products, services and other outputs through:

✗ understanding disruptive trends and competitive forces
✗ providing a range of different industry perspectives
✗ designing experiments for prototyping and testing
✗ measuring the results of those experiments
✗ redesigning the offering to suit stakeholder needs.

Organisations that undervalue the importance of design may be missing significant opportunities. Production costs can be cut for instance, and careful design of the manufacturing process can bring substantial savings. It can also make processes more environmentally conscious and friendly, helping businesses comply with (and hopefully outperform) sustainability regulations and legislation. Designers are in a unique position to employ technical and social skills to push the boundaries and meet business and human needs.

In business, design can enhance the outcomes of numerous innovation activities, from the design of a product to implementing strategies and changing company culture. Internationally, governments have sponsored research to investigate the use of design in the management of creativity. They found that an investment in design can have a significant, positive economic impact on an organisation (UK Design Council, 2008). Recent research has illustrated that design innovation expands beyond design as a physical/tangible outcome to the relationship between the company and its customers, employees and other stakeholders. It is the success of these relationships that determines the uptake and integration of design at a strategic level.

Great ideas need great business plans, great ways to

communicate their value, and a greater understanding of their position within increasingly complex markets. Innovation requires thinking beyond products and mobile applications; it is the creation of value through a novel offering. The term 'innovation' itself is convoluted. Morris (2009) believes that the outcome and process of innovation are often confused, explaining that modest product extensions are often described as innovative. This is incremental change (still a form of innovation) as it relies on existing technologies and business models. However, the types of innovation vary dramatically, and the classification of these types can be easily disputed.

Verganti (2008) explores the role of meaning and innovation in product design, explaining that there are different drivers that lead to incremental and radical innovation. The innovation of meaning is incremental when a product adopts a design language and delivers a message that is in line with current sociocultural models. Users would probably perceive this product as 'fashionable' as it conforms to existing definitions of beauty. The innovation of meaning may also be radical, particularly when a product has a language and delivers a message that implies a significant reinterpretation of its meaning. One example, as detailed by Veganti (2008), is Swatch – who changed the meaning of a watch from a jewel or time instrument to a fashion accessory. Another is the Nintendo Wii, which changed the meaning of home consoles from a platform for dedicated gamers to one that is appealing to non-gamers by being accessible, fun, and interactive.

The discipline of innovation is pushed by a need for new discoveries and strategies to drive growth and survival. For an organisation to be able to innovate, it must evolve, adapt, be flexible, and constantly improve in order to survive and thrive (Keeley et al. 2013). One great idea (or even a not-so-great idea) in isolation is not innovation; it's just an idea or, if implemented, a solution.

INNOVATION, NOT IDEATION!

INNOVATION REQUIRES SMART PEOPLE. INNOVATION SHOULD BE YOUR COMPETITIVE ADVANTAGE, NOT A BUZZWORD OR A COMMODITY THAT SPREADS QUICKLY TO IMITATORS WORLDWIDE.

IDEAS ALONE ARE NOT ENOUGH.

STAKEHOLDERS AND INNOVATION

DESIGN INNOVATION REQUIRES MULTIPLE DISCIPLINES AND THE FREEDOM TO EXPLORE MULTIPLE PERSPECTIVES.

THE VALUE OF DESIGN IN BUSINESS

The use of design principles to inform how your organisation communicates with its customers, creates business partnerships, and develops a collective company culture can be the thread that sews internal, external, strategic and operational management together. One of the main objectives of design is to offer a unique experience to consumers in order to improve the likelihood of their purchasing or repurchasing a product (Chitturi et al., 2008). Companies have learnt that to attain a competitive advantage they cannot solely rely on meeting the functional requirements of the customer. The design of an experience takes the customer beyond products, services, spaces and technology to provide an experience with emotional value; as 'functional benefits alone, it seems, are no longer enough to capture customers or create the brand distinction to retain them' (Brown 2009, 112).

Over the past decade, product designers have become aware of the importance of creating strong emotional relationships intertwined with tangible products. Despite this, the design of business innovation that incorporates emotions is not well understood. We have researched this area for the past several years, through the development of designing emotionally engaging digital experiences (Wrigley & Straker, 2018). Finding that such an approach can offer a powerful competitive advantage as it is almost impossible to replicate.

Joziasse and Selders (2009) identify three key areas of value from design:
✕ ability to handle complex problems
✕ consider the longer-term view
✕ develop a creative approach to addressing strategic problems

The popularity of using a design approach in business has, over the past three decades, evolved to create enterprises that are able to translate intimate customer knowledge into successful product or service offerings (Lojacono & Zaccai, 2004). This development has been written about from theoretical viewpoints (Verganti, 2006; Cooper, Junginger & Lockwood, 2013), and case studies on practical implications have also been published (Martin, 2009; Brown, 2008).

Much has been written about the ability of design to increase productivity, product performance, and emotional connection with customers, but comparatively, little focus has been given to understanding how design can be used to shape a customer or user's latent needs into an organisational strategy. Lojacono and Zaccai (2004, 79) describe design 'as the art and science of putting all the pieces together – technical, financial, operational, and emotional'. We argue that most companies are experts on the technical, financial, and operational aspects of what they do; however, the connection with customers is more mysterious. Most companies conduct surveys, focus groups and questionnaires to understand what their customers want and if they are satisfied. These methods often overlook customers' higher-order needs, desires and aspirations. The key to a design innovation approach is the ability to form insights through a deeper understanding of customer meaning and value, rather than being directed by user requirements. Ikea, Tesco, BMW, Apple and Disney are considered as 'design-led' companies because they have moved from a product-centric view of design to create holistic experiences and services for their customers.

Our book examines design practice from entrepreneurial or intrapreneurial perspectives. The key difference between design entrepreneurs and intrapreneurs is the organisational context in which they are trying to innovate. Each comes with different levels of risks and rewards. Most people understand the term entrepreneur as referring to someone who can source and act upon opportunities: someone who can translate inventions or technologies into products and services that can generate a profit. This is done by launching and running a new business venture. However, the role design plays when used to drive innovation inside an organisation is less understood.

In many cases, intrapreneurs work on projects that foster innovation within their organisation. Such a team might, for instance, explore a new innovative business model that would create a sustainable future for the organisation. Another key difference is that intrapreneurs don't take on the same kind of risks as entrepreneurs; their risk is reputational. So, while it could have consequences for their career, the financial risks associated with entrepreneurship are not there.

A DESIGN ENTREPRENEUR VS INTRAPRENEUR

DESIGN INNOVATION AND DESIGN INTEGRATION

The use of the word design has recently shifted from a noun to a verb, concerned with the application of a problem-solving process rather than referring to the physical features of an object (Walsh, 1996; Wrigley, 2016). The popularisation of and interest in the use of design and design methods for business innovation has grown since the term design thinking was coined.

The notion of using design methods to solve complex problems is not new. During the 1960s Rittel introduced the notion of 'wicked problems' (a problem that is difficult or near impossible to tackle due to a range of factors), and how design as a thinking approach could be used to solve them. Rittel explains that any innovation theory, including design, must not be based on knowledge alone but also on action. The next sections will help you understand the foundations of our discipline, its evolution, and the key authorities who have played a role in its development.

DESIGN THINKING

As the theoretical foundations of Design Innovation and Design Integration are attributed to Design Thinking, we must explore the roots of this construct. Buchanan (1992) argues that the nature (wickedness) of a problem and the primary focus (subject matter) of the design determine the direction of the solution. In some cases a solution may not even exist. But in most case studies of design, many solutions will exist and so, design deals fundamentally with choice. Rittel and Webber (1973) suggest that at the heart of the process of designing is the designer's ability to reason with multiple perspectives and solutions in order to make well-informed choices. The central component of reasoning underpins major models of design thinking both historically and in modern literature (Brown, 2008; Cross, 2006; Martin, 2009; Rowe, 1987; Rylander, 2009; Schön, 1983).

Schön (1983) and Rowe (1987) contributed heavily to an early understanding of the relationship that designers held to their subject matter. Rowe determined that design thinking was a direct articulation of the designer and the act of designing (Rowe, 1987). As an architect or urban designer progressed from one loose sketch to the next, they consciously and subconsciously explored the design problem from multiple perspectives. Schön had earlier proposed that the designer establishes a 'reflection-in-action' conversation with the situation or design problem (Schön, 1983).

Design thinking as a defined approach became a greater feature of scholarly debate during the 1990s and into the turn of the 21st century, accompanying the rapid rise of new technologies and, consequently, new wicked problems, particularly those concerning mass communication. Buchanan (1992) describes design thinking as an approach to complex problem solving which held the ability to generate multiple viable solutions for the same problem. In generating multiple solutions, Buchanan adds that designers must reason with the multiple perspectives of an ideal world (Buchanan, 1995).

Cross (2006) defines design thinking as a cognitive problem-solving process using a unique type of intelligence based on reasoning and logical inference. This cognitive process allows the central activities of design to extend beyond problem solving, to problem identification, solution generation and strategy. Designers problem solve through iterative and emergent approaches, while non-designers are usually analytical and rational (Rylander, 2009). Rylander (2009) presents design thinking as a form of pragmatic inquiry, dealing with alternative interpretations of the same physical reality.

Creativity within the design process is considered central to the designer's ability to frame and reframe the problem at hand (Dorst & Cross, 2001). While Cross refers to the 'creative leap' (a flare of insight that progresses the design), it was not so long ago that Schön described the notion of 'surprise' in creativity that prevented designers from routine behaviour; the type of behaviour that might inhibit original thoughts (Schön, 1983). Dorst further explores framing and reframing problems as an approach enabled by design thinking and describes design thinking as a paradigm for problem solving. Problem-solution framing is critical in determining the different kinds of reasoning, processes and skills that will be used within a design approach (Dorst, 2011).

Thinking large and considering problems within a broader social context opens new avenues for radical innovation enabled by design thinking. Martin defines design thinking as an enabler for transforming knowledge, the core value of a company, into market value – this spans well beyond the general product-centric paradigm that has been traditionally associated with design (Martin, 2009). Indeed, design thinking may also be applied to create new value: top-line growth (increased revenue and profit margins) and the creation of novel strategies by which new competitive advantages can be created. Designers can navigate this complex space as the designer's sensibility and methods are used to generate solutions that are viable, feasible and desirable (Brown, 2008).

Given the scope of debate about design thinking, there is great value in understanding the concept's trajectory over time. Discussion on design thinking began by focusing on the relationship between the designer and design problem, carried out as an articulation of the design activity itself. As a relationship, design thinking described the murky zone between thinking and doing. When this relationship was articulated and understood, the process of design thinking was then grafted into an approach, with design tools and methods provoking thought and action.

Within business spheres, design thinking incorporates design tools and methods that disrupt linear styles and processes of thought to enable novel innovations in strategy, business models and value chain delivery. By nature, these types of innovation are disruptive, thus enabling new competitive advantages. As the field matures, new divergent streams, each defined by their purpose and intended outcome – most notably as a strategic position within business – are now extending design thinking into business practice and government policy.

As you can see, many authorities have commented on the definition of design thinking. Consequently, what design thinking is and how it is practised can vary widely. Scholarly contributions have approached design thinking from three major perspectives. Design thinking as a:

1. cognitive style (Cross, 2006; Dorst, 2011; Rylander, 2009)
2. general design theory (Rittel & Webber, 1973; Rowe, 1987; Schön, 1983)
3. resource (Beckman & Barry, 2008; Brown, 2008; Martin, 2009; Verganti, 2009).

Given the relatively recent emergence of the field, this lack of consensus is not of great surprise. As Rylander (2009) points out, it's hard enough defining the separate activities of design and thinking, let alone design thinking. That design is the adjective before thinking might denote to some extent that design thinking is the property of designers and limited to the design profession. From more simplified viewpoints design thinking broadly describes the approach of designers as they problem solve. But the diversity of today's professional design practice and its new reach into business management make a generic definition of design thinking an impossible fit for all. In a similar vein, discourse on design innovation and design integration presents as an emerging area of academic debate. Design innovation and design integration are two essential and distinctive theoretical fields that describe the process and outcome of the implementation of design thinking within an organisation.

DESIGN INNOVATION

Design innovation represents a set of tools and approaches that enable design thinking to be embedded as a cultural transformation within a business (Bucolo & Matthews, 2011). Design innovation uses methods central to the discipline of design to create product and service solutions that:

✕ are integrated
✕ anticipate future user/customer needs
✕ build future proposals
✕ encourage feedback.

The tools and methods employed in design innovation are based on human-centred principles, which contrasts the typical commercial agenda based on traditional market data. These tools and methods, when properly applied, can be used to interpret and evaluate customers' latent needs, and therefore inform the future products or services that a business may provide.

Market data and stakeholder assumptions held by a business are tested through the engagement of customers using design tools such as personas[3] and narratives[4] (Beckman & Barry, 2008). The insights that emerge from such tools are critical to explore the drivers behind a customer's subconscious and conscious decisions to engage with a business. Through design innovation, a business may also offer unique solutions to the customer based on new meanings – these describe the underlying why that motivates customers and key stakeholders to make conscious and subconscious decisions to purchase or use a particular product or service.

While traditional versions of the design process – steps going from discovery to ideation, design development, and production – are easily incorporated into 'business as usual', design innovation encourages businesses to examine the broader picture beyond a product or service in isolation. This challenges businesses to consider design as a fundamental tool in creating and capturing new knowledge and value, with the possibility of linking this value to the strategic focus of the business. Longstanding conflicts between the differing mindsets held by design and business professionals can prevent the integration of design as a mindset and approach within business (Bucolo & Matthews, 2011; Lee & Evans, 2012). The resolution of this conflict may lie in the creation of a role focused on bridging conceptual work and practice. Such a role (a design catalyst) is presented and discussed later in the book.

Designers are increasingly encouraged to transition from designing products and services to designing business models that are supportive of radical innovations. Aesthetic and functional innovations at a product level are no longer providing competitive advantage; such is the competitive nature and product saturation of the global marketplace. However, a common product or service accompanied by a

[3] Personas are representations of target stakeholders that are formed out of insights and themes that can be uncovered through user research.

[4] A story written by a designer that can be used to help communicate a scenario, or to test ideas and assumptions.

radically innovative business model may be more successful than a radically innovative product or service accompanied by a poor business model (Chesbrough, 2010).

Product success has been associated with a product's relationship to an attached service (such as the famous Apple products and the Genius Bar). This highlights the value of linking products and services to a supportive business model. The tools of design innovation allow for the radical redesign of business models through iterative testing with customers and stakeholders, prompting business to consider the broader context of the opportunities and challenges that may be faced. A company has achieved design integration when it embeds a design thinking culture and philosophy to create new value across all aspects of the business.

Bennet (2011) argues that design integration as a theory is important to the growth of the discipline into new contexts that extend beyond the traditional design studio setting. In isolation, the term integration describes bringing together parts to create a whole or mixing foreign parts to make a new collective (Gulledge, 2006). Design integration, in the traditional design literature, describes the multidisciplinary collaboration that occurs when bringing an idea from plan to completion by linking stakeholders (Quatman & Dhar, 2003). Here, we refer to design integration as the synthesis of design as a problem-solving and value-creating philosophy at each layer of a business's value chain based on its vision for growth.

Design has traditionally been integrated into business through new product development, graphic design, environmental design and marketing (Borja de Mozota, 2002). The interpretation of an initial design brief and the implementation of this brief through build or manufacturing stages demand the designer to manage multiple parties. The core skills of collaboration and managing expectations are central to the designer. These skills are integral when design shifts from a project level to the management and strategic realms of business.

One way of understanding the degree to which design is integrated in an organisation is the Danish Design Ladder. This framework was developed as part of the Danish Design Council's policy to boost innovation through the adoption

DESIGN INTEGRATION

of design. It details the steps necessary for the integration of design at a strategic level (Kretzschmar, 2003). The design ladder steps from no use of design within a business to the: use of design in the consideration of form, integration of design within the early stages of new developments, and integration of design within the business's strategy. Thus, this prominent framework offers a clear and tangible method for gauging the extent to which design is used in an organisation.

Top-down design leadership is critical in driving the integration of design with all stakeholders and aspects of a business (Lee & Evans, 2012). Without strong leadership, the integration of design loses strength and fails to disseminate widely within a business's value chain. An emotionally intelligent and empathic leader may also increase the likelihood of the creative and innovative environment necessary for the adoption of design (Isaksen & Akkermans; 2011). The disconnect between dominant business disciplines and the discipline of design and its perceived value typically acts as a barrier to the integration of design into business culture (Drews, 2009; Matthews, Bucolo, & Wrigley, 2012). Full integration of design beyond its traditional project-level setting into business management meets many challenges, with these varying based on the size of the business, the industry in which it operates, as well as other cultural and environmental factors.

WHERE TO NEXT?

With the increased use of design comes the challenge of ensuring 'design innovation' remains innovative; by definition, innovation can only exist in a continuum, defined not only by what comes before it but by how it is received (Erlhoff & Marshall, 2007). An important distinction of the design innovation process is that it is not only a problem-solving approach – as design thinking suggests – but also a transformational process at the business level. The conservative role designers perform in the innovation process within a business is increasingly being challenged, with an increasing emphasis on the value design can bring to an organisation. Martin (2007) has published widely on the relationship between design and business, asking the key question: 'why can't business and design be friends?'. He makes it clear that business is centred on reliability, while design is focused on validity – and this conflict between the two approaches creates tension. This tension can be used as a way to appreciate legitimate differences and perspectives between the two. It is well known that constraints can lead to good design (Norman, 1999). With this in mind, working in the parameters of these two fields should then, too, lead to good outcomes that span reliability and validity. Thankfully, designers have many tools to assist with just such an endeavour.

2020 YEARS OF DESIGN &INNOVATION

 Date of famous innovators & innovations

 Birth year of 'must know' designers (go on add yourself in)

Seminial work in research (all references included at the back of the book)

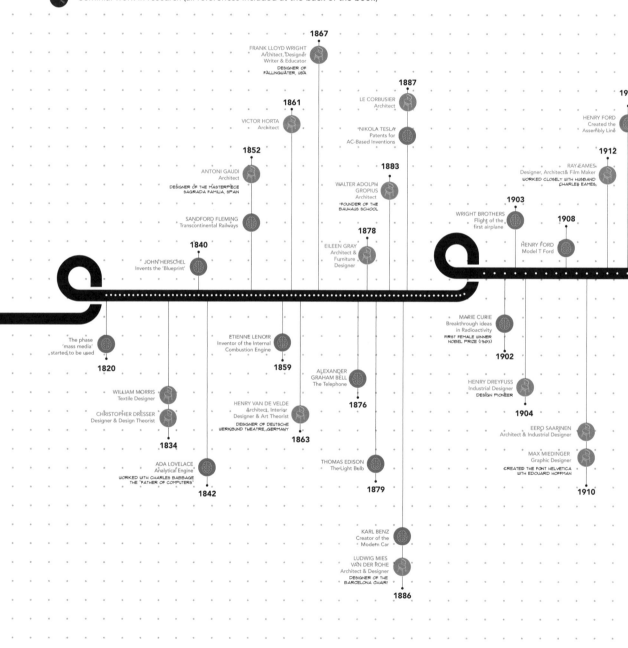

1867
FRANK LLOYD WRIGHT
Architect, Designer
Writer & Educator
DESIGNER OF
FALLINGWATER, USA

1887
LE CORBUSIER
Architect

1913
HENRY FORD
Created the
Assembly Line

1861
VICTOR HORTA
Architect

NIKOLA TESLA
Patents for
AC-Based Inventions

1912
RAY EAMES
Designer, Architect & Film Maker
WORKED CLOSELY WITH HUSBAND
CHARLES EAMES

1852
ANTONI GAUDI
Architect
DESIGNER OF THE MASTERPIECE
SAGRADA FAMILIA, SPAIN

1883
WALTER ADOLPH
GROPIUS
Architect
FOUNDER OF THE
BAUHAUS SCHOOL

SANDFORD FLEMING
Transcontinental Railways

1903
WRIGHT BROTHERS
Flight of the
first airplane

1908
HENRY FORD
Model T Ford

1878
EILEEN GRAY
Architect &
Furniture
Designer

1840
JOHN HERSCHEL
Invents the 'Blueprint'

The phase
'mass media'
started to be used

MARIE CURIE
Breakthrough ideas
in Radioactivity
FIRST FEMALE WINNER
NOBEL PRIZE (1903)

1820

ÉTIENNE LENOIR
Inventor of the Internal
Combustion Engine

1902

1859

ALEXANDER
GRAHAM BELL
The Telephone

HENRY DREYFUSS
Industrial Designer
DESIGN PIONEER

WILLIAM MORRIS
Textile Designer

1876

1904

CHRISTOPHER DRESSER
Designer & Design Theorist

HENRY VAN DE VELDE
Architect, Interior
Designer & Art Theorist
DESIGNER OF DEUTSCHE
WERKBUND THEATRE, GERMANY

EERO SAARINEN
Architect & Industrial Designer

1834

1863

MAX MIEDINGER
Graphic Designer
CREATED THE FONT HELVETICA
WITH EDOUARD HOFFMAN

ADA LOVELACE
Analytical Engine
WORKED WITH CHARLES BABBAGE
THE 'FATHER OF COMPUTERS'

THOMAS EDISON
The Light Bulb

1842

1879

1910

KARL BENZ
Creator of the
Modern Car

LUDWIG MIES
VAN DER ROHE
Architect & Designer
DESIGNER OF THE
BARCELONA CHAIR!

1886

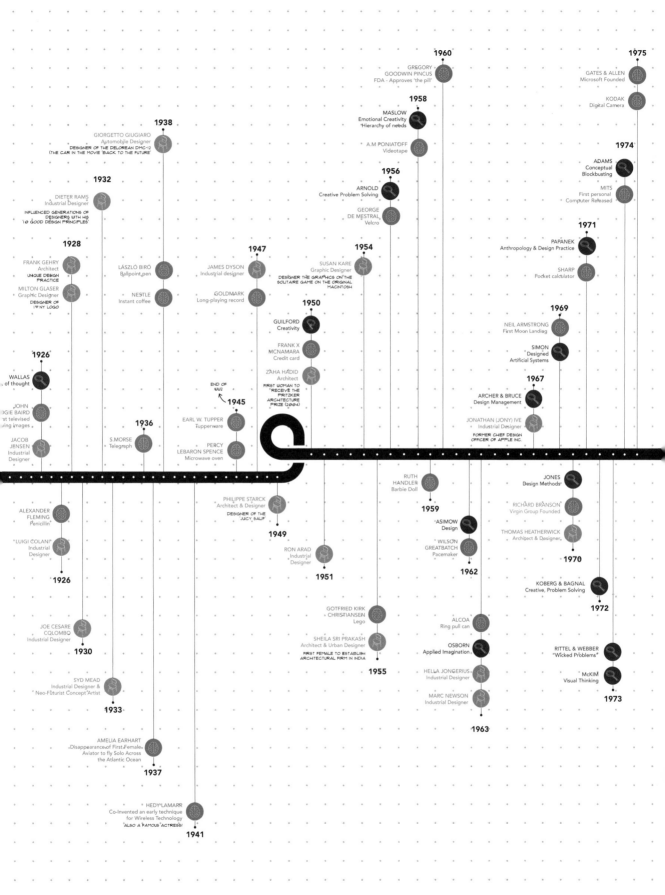

1960
GREGORY
GOODWIN PINCUS
FDA - Approves 'the pill'

1975
GATES & ALLEN
Microsoft Founded

KODAK
Digital Camera

1958
MASLOW
Emotional Creativity
'Hierarchy of needs'

A.M PONIATOFF
Videotape

1974
ADAMS
Conceptual
Blockbusting

MITS
First personal
Computer Released

1938
GIORGETTO GIUGIARO
Automobile Designer
DESIGNER OF THE DELOREAN DMC-12
(THE CAR IN THE MOVIE 'BACK TO THE FUTURE'

1956
ARNOLD
Creative Problem Solving

GEORGE
DE MESTRAL
Velcro

1932
DIETER RAMS
Industrial Designer
INFLUENCED GENERATIONS OF
DESIGNERS WITH HIS
'10 GOOD DESIGN PRINCIPLES'

1971
PAPANEK
Anthropology & Design Practice

SHARP
Pocket calculator

1928
FRANK GEHRY
Architect
UNIQUE DESIGN
PRACTICE

MILTON GLASER
Graphic Designer
DESIGNER OF
I ♥ NY LOGO

LÁSZLÓ BIRÓ
Ballpoint pen

NESTLE
Instant coffee

1947
JAMES DYSON
Industrial designer

GOLDMARK
Long-playing record

1954
SUSAN KARE
Graphic Designer
DESIGNER THE GRAPHICS ON THE
SOLITAIRE GAME ON THE ORIGINAL
MACINTOSH

1950
GUILFORD
Creativity

FRANK X
MCNAMARA
Credit card

1969
NEIL ARMSTRONG
First Moon Landing

SIMON
Designed
Artificial Systems

1926
WALLAS
of thought

JOHN
OGIE BAIRD
st televised
ving images

JACOB
JENSEN
Industrial
Designer

S.MORSE
Telegraph

1936

ZAHA HADID
Architect
FIRST WOMAN TO
RECEIVE THE
PRITZKER
ARCHITECTURE
PRIZE (2004)

END OF
WW2

1945

EARL W. TUPPER
Tupperware

PERCY
LEBARON SPENCE
Microwave oven

1967
ARCHER & BRUCE
Design Management

JONATHAN (JONY) IVE
Industrial Designer
FORMER CHIEF DESIGN
OFFICER OF APPLE INC.

RUTH
HANDLER
Barbie Doll

JONES
Design Methods

1959

ALEXANDER
FLEMING
Penicillin

PHILIPPE STARCK
Architect & Designer
DESIGNER OF THE
'JUICY SALIF'

1949

RICHARD BRANSON
Virgin Group Founded

THOMAS HEATHERWICK
Architect & Designer

1970

'LUIGI COLANI'
Industrial
Designer

RON ARAD
Industrial
Designer

1951

ASIMOW
Design

WILSON
GREATBATCH
Pacemaker

1962

1926

KOBERG & BAGNAL
Creative, Problem Solving

1972

JOE CESARE
COLOMBO
Industrial Designer

1930

GOTFRIED KIRK
CHRISTIANSEN
Lego

SHEILA SRI PRAKASH
Architect & Urban Designer
FIRST FEMALE TO ESTABLISH
ARCHITECTURAL FIRM IN INDIA

1955

ALCOA
Ring pull can

OSBORN
Applied Imagination

RITTEL & WEBBER
"Wicked Problems"

McKIM
Visual Thinking

1973

SYD MEAD
Industrial Designer &
Neo-Futurist Concept Artist

1933

HELLA JONGERIUS
Industrial Designer

MARC NEWSON
Industrial Designer

1963

AMELIA EARHART
Disappearance of First Female
Aviator to fly Solo Across
the Atlantic Ocean

1937

HEDY LAMARR
Co-Invented an early technique
for Wireless Technology
'ALSO A FAMOUS ACTRESS'

1941

31

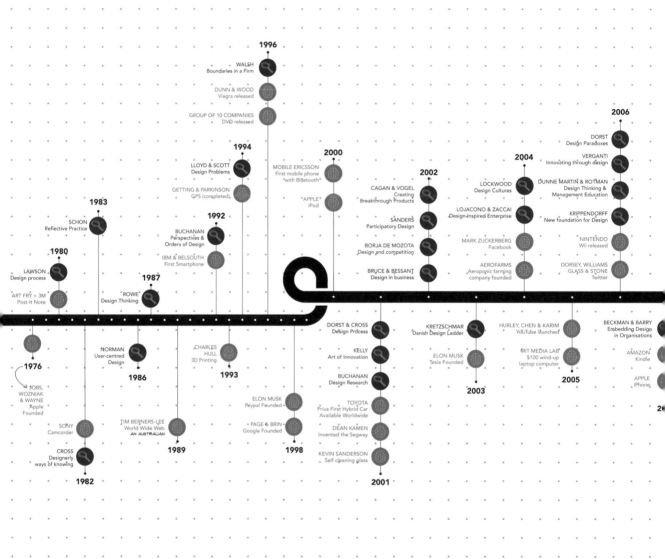

1996
WALSH
Boundaries in a Firm

DUNN & WOOD
Viagra released

GROUP OF 10 COMPANIES
DVD released

1994
LLOYD & SCOTT
Design Problems

GETTING & PARKINSON
GPS (completed)

1992
BUCHANAN
Perspectives &
Orders of Design

IBM & BELSOUTH
First Smartphone

1983
SCHON
Reflective Practice

1980
LAWSON
Design process

ART FRY + 3M
Post-It Note

1987
ROWE
Design Thinking

MOBILE ERICSSON
First mobile phone
"with Bluetooth"

2000
APPLE
iPod

CAGAN & VOGEL
Creating
Breakthrough Products

2002
SANDERS
Participatory Design

BORJA DE MOZOTA
Design and competition

BRUCE & BESSANT
Design in business

LOCKWOOD
Design Cultures

2004
DUNNE MARTIN & ROTMAN
Design Thinking &
Management Education

LOJACONO & ZACCAI
Design-Inspired Enterprise

MARK ZUCKERBERG
Facebook

AEROFARMS
Aeroponic farming
company founded

2006
DORST
Design Paradoxes

VERGANTI
Innovating through design

KRIPPENDORFF
New foundation for Design

NINTENDO
Wii released

DORSEY, WILLIAMS
GLASS & STONE
Twitter

NORMAN
User-centred
Design

1986

CHARLES
HULL
3D Printing

1993

1976

JOBS,
WOZNIAK
& WAYNE
Apple
Founded

SONY
Camcorder

CROSS
Designerly
ways of knowing

1982

TIM BERNERS-LEE
World Wide Web
AN AUSTRALIAN

1989

ELON MUSK
Peypal Founded

PAGE & BRIN
Google Founded

1998

DORST & CROSS
Design Process

KELLY
Art of Innovation

BUCHANAN
Design Research

TOYOTA
Prius First Hybrid Car
Available Worldwide

DEAN KAMEN
Invented the Segway

KEVIN SANDERSON
Self cleaning glass

2001

KRETZSCHMAR
Danish Design Ladder

ELON MUSK
Tesla Founded

2003

HURLEY, CHEN & KARIM
YouTube launched

MIT MEDIA LAB
$100 wind-up
laptop computer

2005

BECKMAN & BARRY
Embedding Design
in Organisations

AMAZON
Kindle

APPLE
iPhone

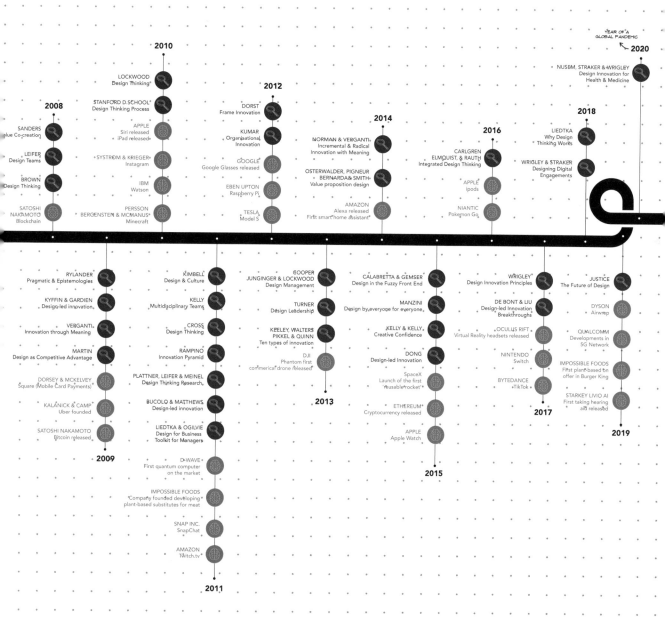

YEAR OF A
GLOBAL PANDEMIC
2020

2010

LOCKWOOD
Design Thinking

NUSEM, STRAKER & WRIGLEY
Design Innovation for
Health & Medicine

STANFORD D.SCHOOL
Design Thinking Process

2012

2008

DORST
Frame Innovation

2018

SANDERS
Value Co-creation

APPLE
Siri released
iPad released

KUMAR
Organisational
Innovation

2014

LIEDTKA
Why Design
Thinking Works

LEIFER
Design Teams

SYSTROM & KRIEGER
Instagram

NORMAN & VERGANTI
Incremental & Radical
Innovation with Meaning

2016

WRIGLEY & STRAKER
Designing Digital
Engagements

BROWN
Design Thinking

GOOGLE
Google Glasses released

CARLGREN
ELMQUIST, & RAUTH
Integrated Design Thinking

IBM
Watson

OSTERWALDER, PIGNEUR
BERNARDA& SMITH
Value proposition design

SATOSHI
NAKAMOTO
Blockchain

PERSSON
BERGENSTEN & MCMANUS
Minecraft

EBEN UPTON
Raspberry Pi

APPLE
ipods

AMAZON
Alexa released
First smart home assistant

NIANTIC
Pokemon Go

TESLA
Model S

RYLANDER
Pragmatic & Epistemologies

KIMBELL
Design & Culture

COOPER
JUNGINGER & LOCKWOOD
Design Management

CALABRETTA & GEMSER
Design in the Fuzzy Front End

WRIGLEY
Design Innovation Principles

JUSTICE
The Future of Design

KYFFIN & GARDIEN
Design-led innovation

KELLY
Multidisciplinary Teams

TURNER
Design Leadership

MANZINI
Design by everyone for everyone

DE BONT & LIU
Design-led Innovation
Breakthroughs

DYSON
Airwrap

VERGANTI
Innovation through Meaning

CROSS
Design Thinking

KEELEY, WALTERS
PIKKEL & QUINN
Ten types of innovation

KELLY & KELLY
Creative Confidence

OCULUS RIFT
Virtual Reality headsets released

QUALCOMM
Developments in
5G Network

MARTIN
Design as Competitive Advantage

RAMPINO
Innovation Pyramid

DJI
Phantom first
commerical drone released

DONG
Design-led Innovation

NINTENDO
Switch

IMPOSSIBLE FOODS
First plant-based on
offer in Burger King

DORSEY & MCKELVEY
Square (Mobile Card Payments)

PLATTNER, LEIFER & MEINEL
Design Thinking Research

2013

SpaceX
Launch of the first
'reusable' rocket

BYTEDANCE
TikTok

STARKEY LIVIO AI
First taking hearing
aid released

KALANICK & CAMP
Uber founded

BUCOLO & MATTHEWS
Design-led innovation

ETHEREUM
Cryptocurrency released

2017

SATOSHI NAKAMOTO
Bitcoin released

LIEDTKA & OGILVIE
Design for Business
Toolkit for Managers

APPLE
Apple Watch

2019

2009

D-WAVE
First quantum computer
on the market

2015

IMPOSSIBLE FOODS
Company founded developing
plant-based substitutes for meat

SNAP INC.
SnapChat

AMAZON
Twitch.tv

2011

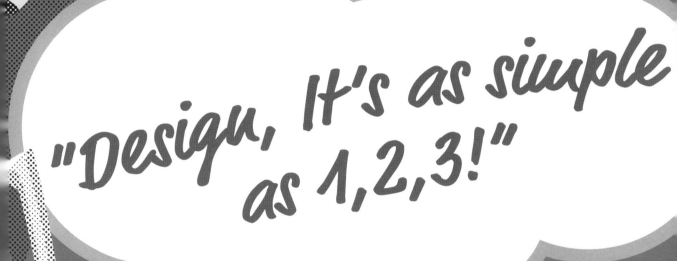

"Design, It's as simple as 1, 2, 3!"

If it was a fool proof process wouldn't we have more amazing products, services and solutions? Why hasn't the 'empathise' step solved all our problems? We have all been guilty at one point or another of buying into the five-step plan to financial success or the three easy steps to lose weight today. Placing anything into a 'step' process is a selling tool – it makes things look easy and simple. However, creative processes cannot be carried out in a rigid set of steps. Designers are good at dealing with uncertainty or revisiting square one – not to say it's not frustrating, but we are okay with it.

DESIGN TOOLS

IT'S NOT ALL
ABOUT THE TOOLS

Many design tools exist. In fact, many design toolkits repurpose the same traditional design tools in different combinations, scaffolded by a different 4, 5 or 6-step model. There are many out there, such as Kumar's (2012), which outlines 101 different design methods (tools or approaches) to innovate, ranging from exploring concepts to reframing insights. Or the seminal work derived by the Delft Design Guide, which presents an overview of a product design approach and aligning methods. Many of the tools outlined in such texts are presented visually, meaning they require the participant or user of the tool to fill out a worksheet or draw relationships between items.

Liedtka and Ogilvie (2011) also presents 10 tools for design thinking, which are targeted at managers and used frequently as textbooks in MBA programs globally to find and pursue innovation and growth in a business context. This builds upon earlier work from Sarasvathy (2001) who established effectuation – a way of thinking that assists entrepreneurs in the processes of opportunity identification and new venture creation. Effectuation includes a set of decision-making principles that Sarasvathy claims to be the ultimate selection mechanism for successful innovation. Sarasvathy (2001) proclaims that causation is the opposite of effectuation. While effectuation is used in situations of uncertainty, causal reasoning is used when the future is predictable. Situations of uncertainty are described as when the future is unpredictable, and goals are not clearly known.

Design tools (in particular canvases or templates) are simplified in order to be useful. The more complicated they are the more they get in the way (or become the focal point instead of the problem or purpose for the tool in the first place). The success of the Business Model Canvas by Osterwalder and Pigneur (2010) as a tool, for example, is due to its simplicity; it allows the user to visualise a business model and constantly iterate through simple but powerful communication.

As we previously said, design tools are meant to be designed, broken, reformed, merged and reinvented for every process and project, all depending on the aim of the task at hand. Take for instance personas – a well-documented and respected tool that is part of most designers' repertoires. A persona is a character that is used to represent typical groups of users, customers or other stakeholders. They can be constructed based on real data or can be complete works of fiction. If you look at how personas are used in industry (or do a quick search of examples), you will see that the vast majority – if not all the examples – focus on user personas. While there is nothing wrong with that, it does little to illustrate the broad range of applications for most design tools when you apply just a little creative thinking.

To illustrate this point, we will take you through two adaptations of personas that our team uses: manager personas and reverse personas. A manager persona can be used to identify key leadership and management styles, and behavioural and cultural characteristics. This type of information allows executive management or a senior leader to identify who could trial, launch and roll out a new product or service within an organisation (Straker, Mosely and Wrigley, 2019). This flips the usual orientation of a persona from one that is external to the organisation (such as a user), to one that is internal (such as an employee or manager). The content is also a little different, for instance by focusing on business goals rather than life goals – which can facilitate the persona being used as a strategic aid, and not just as a design and communication aid which is the general use of personas. Similarly, the reverse persona can be used to personify an organisation and provide insight into aspects like risk aversion and capacity for change. Its primary purpose is a tool for communication, which is accomplished through a combination of analogies and facts about the organisation (e.g., an organisation which is slow to change might be captured through an individual which is well acquainted with the snooze button). This can help a designer facilitate a difficult conversation around an organisation's less desirable qualities in an indirect, non-accusatory way. Hopefully, these two examples illustrate how a simple alteration can fundamentally change the purpose and application of a design tool. Design tools are not rigid, and you need to be comfortable with adapting them.

When using design tools, this flexibility and ability to adapt can very quickly identify and separate the novice from the expert. The expert will use their design intuition and training to address the problem at hand. While the novice will rely solely on the tool to scaffold the task. This isn't to say that a scaffold isn't useful. It provides a solid place to start and a familiar, intuitive tool can have notable benefits:

✗ Design tools can help facilitate organisation-wide communication. This includes communication of input and feedback loops, alongside cataloguing and documenting the innovation project itself. Tools can assist the process of both acquiring information and disseminating it as feedback. Another aspect of facilitating communication is recording and filing information about a project's progress. Tools are very good at cataloguing and documenting points in time; if you merge the results together to reflect a project history it can be extremely useful. When going through a design process, you could bring out the previously filled in design tools at the beginning of the workshop or meeting; and then the new one at its conclusion. This can be used to communicate how an idea might have changed and evolved.

✗ Design tools can empower stakeholders to be comfortable contributing to design. The process of starting a conversation about change can be challenging. Especially when talking about the future of a company. However, design tools are useful in empowering stakeholders to grapple with this challenge. They can help individuals, who can sometimes struggle to articulate what they are thinking, to put their ideas forward. Of particular note is the accessibility afforded by the use of visual tools (which can be easily written on and contributed to). However, this is not to say that the process is easy. People can easily get caught up with just 'filling in the boxes', resulting in analytical thinking.

✗ Design tools can facilitate teaching and learning. Teaching employees how to use tools can shift the roles of the designer from a facilitator to a trainer, and can be an excellent method for sharing key insights from a project with the broader organisation. This is a vital step in building design knowledge in an organisation, and a requisite for design integration (which can't happen if only a few individuals are familiar with design and capable of practicing it). Doing design with an organisation rather than for them, and focusing on teaching and learning, can make stakeholders in the organisation aware of design and guide them to collaboratively address problems in their own business units.

While tools can facilitate a design approach, tools alone do not hold all the answers. They have many strengths- including synthesising and framing information (or insights), provide a way to communicate across business departments, to engage and ignite creative thinking with employees, and facilitate further teaching and learning throughout a business. What is important to recognise is that the role of the designer is just as important, if not more important, than the tool itself. You must be capable of bending the rules, changing a tool's purpose, and adapting it to a companies' needs spontaneously. Although many tools are provided with instructions, they still require the facilitation and mindset of a designer to provide their full value.

A QUICK SIDENOTE

Designers are very good at claiming that they can solve any problem. A lot of designers might be willing to give anything a go, but it might be that design is not the best or most appropriate approach to take. Before engaging designers (or using design), first you must ask: is this approach the correct one for the context and problem at hand? A designer might be well equipped to identify an issue or problem, but are they best suited to finding a solution?

For instance, a technical problem might well be better suited to an engineer (for understanding mechanical stress in a product) or programmer (for a software glitch). [5] A designer could be a huge asset in identifying policy change, but realising this change is going to be a team effort that will require the expertise of a number of disciplines. Designers themselves are also not all equal. Some might be well-acquainted with products, and others with services. Just because you might know how to 'design' does not make you an expert in every discipline or equip you to solve every problem. Knowing your limitations is just as important as knowing your strengths.

WRAP UP ON DESIGN TOOLS

[5] An industrial designer could likely help with the first example, and someone versed with design computing could tackle the second. However, not all designers have these skills. They are highly technical skills and require specialisation. A more clear-cut example is surgery. A designer could help design the tool required to perform a medical task, but they are poorly equipped to actually perform surgery.

DESIGN
INNOV

DESIGN INNOVATION

Design is the evolution of information (Ullman, 2009). This evolution usually begins with an ill-defined need for a solution and ends with exact specifications for that solution's production and use. The process here is non-linear; it uses abductive and deductive reasoning in what can be described as an intuitive approach. There is no 'one-size-fits-all' process or model.

The highly popular framework of the design thinking process by IDEO (empathise, define, ideate, prototype and test) and its many variations are a great way to articulate the process of designing to non-designers. However, it is naïve to assume that simply following the steps and tools of a design process will always yield innovative outcomes. No model, method, or buzzword will ever be the complete answer – the designer is as important as the design process, so it largely depends on you (the practitioner). For most designers, the relationship between each phase isn't clear-cut; as they are constantly moving between them. Knowing when to move to the next phase and determining which phase should be next is the most crucial part – this is best informed by one's intuition. It depends on you knowing what the best approach is for the context (or trusting that you do) and which methods will achieve the optimal outcome(s). Experienced designers understand the strengths and weaknesses of a design approach, and tailor their approach based on experience and intuition.

We have witnessed many design teams within organisations assign clear deadlines and metrics to each phase. This robs design teams, particularly novice ones, of their creativity and ability to adapt, experiment and discover. These are all key aspects of design. We fear that such processes will set precedent and the expectation that design is predictable, fixed and linear. It is for these reasons that our framework is not comprised of stages, phases or steps to be used in a rigid manner. The components are included and structured

42

for pedagogical purposes, so that you first understand, apply, and then redesign them to suit you and your project requirements. Each component is built upon design, business, and management theories and practices in the attempt to help you conceive and implement innovative solutions. As explained in our previous work (Nusem, Straker & Wrigley, 2020), the design innovation framework is a cognitive approach of conscious and considered actions and choices, featuring six components:

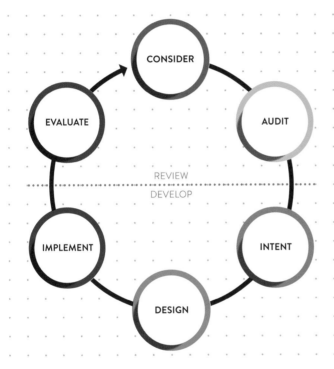

The components should empower you to approach traditional business practices in an experimental and creative way, question your assumptions, collect insights from staff and customers, and to translate these insights into meaningful strategic and operational decisions. The components are provided to form the foundations of what is required within an organisation to better explore, understand and implement creative solutions in a range of complex contexts. They should not limit you to 'what should be done' but inspire you to question 'what else' could be done.

You will notice that one of the components is titled 'design': this is a conscious effort to showcase that design is a part of a larger picture. Design requires lead-up work done before, and significant scoping after, for an idea to become a reality. These facets are often overlooked in design processes; design, as some frameworks might lead you to believe, is not just about problem or needs identification, ideating possible solutions and presenting recommendations. It is also not a process, but the practice of understanding details. These details are often missed or simply forgotten when following step-by-step instructions that provide a means to an end. If you use it as a linear, step-by-step 'process' you have probably missed the point.

A successful design innovation project is not one that works flawlessly, but one that teaches you and the organisation something new about objectives, processes or purpose. Such a project:

✗ has the ability to broaden perspectives, and is a means for discovering opportunities
✗ requires multiple disciplines (such as design and business) to work and evolve together
✗ allows project members to challenge 'business as usual'
✗ can create many different concepts quickly, allowing various scenarios to be prototyped and tested
✗ can facilitate iterative learning and expose whole organisations to new approaches
✗ can be done quickly and inexpensively.

By this stage you have been guided through the theoretical evolution of design, design thinking and innovation, along with a somewhat-practical understanding as we have outlined so far in this chapter. In the following sections we introduce the six components of design innovation in more detail by providing an overview, elaborating on the components and presenting key driving questions to help direct your next design project. Each component is accompanied by a core aspect and a set of example tools. These communicate the focus you should maintain while undertaking each respective component. An overview of the components, core aspects, example tools and methods (we have included blank templates included at the back) and other useful resources are detailed on the next page..

Component	Core Aspect	Methods/Tools	Existing tools, methods and further reading
			(that can also be used but not included in this book)
Consider	Stakeholders	✗ Organisational Conditions Framework ✗ Stakeholder Map	✗ SWOT ✗ PESTLE ✗ Popular Media Scan[a] ✗ Buzz Reports[a] ✗ Trends Matrix[a] ✗ From...To exploration[a] ✗ Futuring Methods
Audit	Insights	✗ Business Model Content Analysis ✗ Customer Segment Profiles ✗ Market Disruptors ✗ Business Model Swot ✗ Plot The Competition ✗ Segmenting Customers ✗ Product Analysis	✗ Business Model Canvas[b] ✗ 10 Types of Innovation[c] ✗ Personas ✗ Competitor Analysis ✗ Network Activity Map[a] ✗ Insight Sorting[a] ✗ Ven Diagramming[a] ✗ Insights Clustering Matrix[a] ✗ User Journey Map[d]
Intent	Value	✗ Value Definition ✗ Customer Design Brief	✗ Value Proposition[b] ✗ Vision Statement ✗ Value Hypothesis ✗ Principles to Opportunities ✗ Design Archetypes
Design	Skills	✗ Defining Your Philosophy ✗ Visualise Your Practice ✗ Design Criteria ✗ Solution Evaluation ✗ Designing Innovative Products ✗ Circle Creation ✗ Innovation Mashing ✗ Mr Squiggle ✗ Post-It Note Pictionary ✗ Letters And Numbers ✗ Prototype Plan	✗ Stand on the shoulders of giants! Read the Delft Design Guide – it outlines many tools, methods and approaches used in a design process
Implement	Communication	✗ Pitching ✗ Business Cases ✗ Product Classification Matrix ✗ 3 Horizons ✗ Johnson & Jones Matrix	✗ Activity Network Mapping ✗ Stage-Gate System ✗ Strategy Roadmap ✗ Pilot Development and Testing[a]
Evaluation	Metrics	✗ ALL OF THE ABOVE but use in an analytical way	✗ Traditional Financial Metrics ✗ ROI Calculations ✗ CRM ✗ Customer Satisfaction Ratings ✗ Traditional Market Research Methods

[a] Kumar, V. (2013). 101 design methods : a structured approach for driving innovation in your organization. Hoboken, New Jersey: Wiley.
[b] Osterwalder, A., & Pigneur, Y. (2010). Business Model Generation: A Handbook for Visionaries, Game Changers, and Challengers. Hoboken, New Jersey: Wiley.
[c] Keeley, L. (2013). Ten Types of Innovation: The Discipline of Building Breakthroughs. Hoboken, New Jersey: Wiley.
[d] Van Boeijen, A., Daalhuizen, J., van der Schoor, R., & Zijlstra, J. (2014). Delft design guide: Design strategies and methods. BIS Publishers.

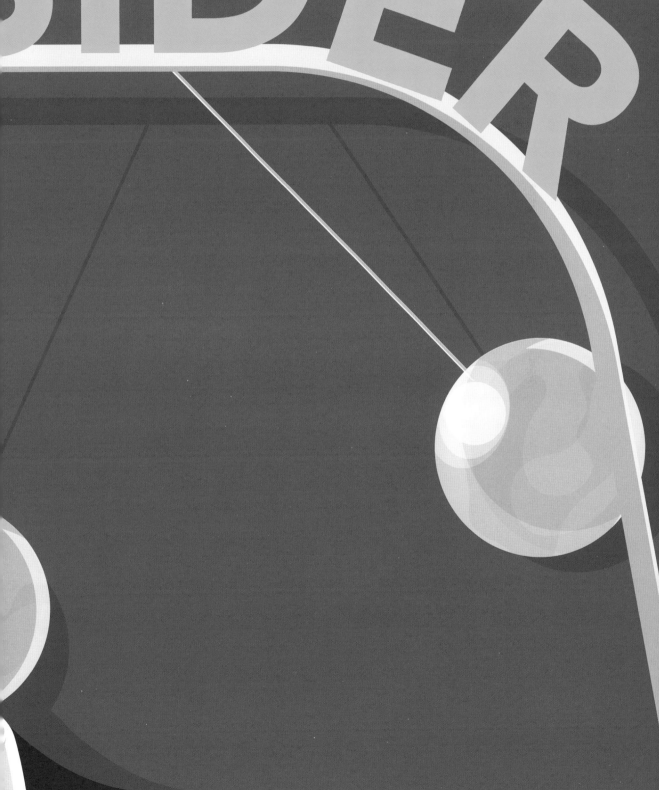

CONSIDER

Design influences and is influenced by a myriad of factors that are dependent on its context. Context is the main focus of **CONSIDER**, the first component of design innovation. Design that is not sensitive to this context is prone to failure (Schön, 1988). For example, an architectural design that does not consider the site plan is unlikely to appropriately fit its context for lighting, ventilation and a host of other factors. The efforts of an individual seeking to redesign the user interface for the SAT exam without realising that the exam is scheduled to change in a few months (as it does every few years) are likely to become redundant (Dubin, 2018). These are failures of context, which need to be thoroughly considered for a design to be rooted in the real world.

When we refer to context, we are describing:
- ✗ archaeology for the specific design and its market (i.e., whether any existing or legacy designs that will influence how a design is perceived and adopted) (Dorst, 2015);
- ✗ the entity practising the design (e.g., a start-up or mature organisation, government entity, etc.) (Wrigley, Nusem, & Straker, 2020)
- ✗ the ecosystem in which the design is intended to be employed (i.e., laws, regulatory bodies, key social groups, etc.) (Rehman & Yan, 2011);

The consider component of the design innovation is, quite simply, about understanding the context in which design is taking place. Considering the three factors listed is a prerequisite of successful design and can help to determine not only the direction for design, but the key barriers to implementation, adoption and success.

Prior to commencing any form of project or design work it is important to consider the conditions that exist for design within the practising entity (i.e. the organisation responsible for the design). A number of texts describe the ideal conditions for design (Mutanen, 2008; Nusem, Wrigley, & Matthews, 2017), whether in organisations or larger government bodies. Ensuring that the right conditions are present, or establishing these conditions, is integral and the first step of the process outlined in this chapter (if you are practicing design within an organisation – this is less relevant for a conceptual design or a start-up). The conditions include strategic vision, directive(s), cultural capital and facilities and are described in detail later in this book. Design lacking internal support through the right conditions may not come to fruition. In addition, if there is ambition for design to continue beyond the immediate project being considered, then failing to establish the correct organisational conditions will jeopardise the long-term success of design within the organisation (Wrigley et al., 2020).

SEE ORGANISATIONAL CONDITIONS PG. 166

Archaeology refers to the influence of previous designs and ways of thinking. It encompasses the maturity of the market or concept, and/or societal understandings or expectations of the design (Dorst, 2015). People have preconceived notions of products and services, and it can be difficult to change these. Affordances and conventions[6] exist for a reason, and it is generally best to acknowledge them (Norman, 1999). This isn't to say that these can't be challenged, only that it is unwise to do so blindly. Things are usually the way they are for a reason. These factors should be considered during the inception of a concept, as they will influence how your design is perceived and interacted with.

The final context is the ecosystem, which represents the external conditions or environment in which one is designing. External conditions vary based on the industry, but are generally composed of regulatory constraints, system requirements, emerging market trends and ethics. Essentially, these external conditions form stage gates (which require some form of formal or informal approval) for the translation of design.

Failing to consider the context can result in a design not receiving the support required or failing to meet regulatory constraints. Understanding the context of use and major stakeholders during initial stages of development can highlight whether the design has merit and whether it should proceed. Designs that do not acknowledge these factors often fail or don't function as intended.

[6] According to Norman (1999), affordances are properties of the world that reflect the possible relationships between actors (people) and objects. Conversely, conventions are arbitrary, artificial, and learned. They can help us master the intricacies of everyday life (e.g., conventions for manners, writing style or operating a computer). As designers we can invent new affordances, but will find it difficult to challenge established social conventions. As a designer you will need to know the difference and exploit it.

STAKEHOLDERS

CORE
STAKEHOLDERS

Context can be understood through the multiple perspectives of **STAKEHOLDERS** for a given design. Investigating these perspectives is therefore a core component of **CONSIDER**. Stakeholder engagement is integral to an organisation's success (Noland & Phillips, 2010). This is equally true for design. Design management literature identifies the satisfaction of stakeholders as a key indicator for innovation, as well as being a contributor to other important factors like time to market, and research and development (Borja de Mozota, 2002). These stakeholders – which Freeman (1984, 46) defines as "any group or individual who can affect or is affected by the achievement of the organisation's objectives" are unsurprisingly of relevance to designers. Engaging with stakeholders will ultimately make the deliverables of design more meaningful to the people who will benefit from them (Sanders, 2002). There are, at the least, seven categories of stakeholders (Mendelow, 1981; Wallace, 1995):

✗ Government – the most formal stakeholder, which embodies the laws and regulations that represent public and business interests. This frames the guidelines for conducting business, as well as the regulatory agencies that control business practices.

✗ Shareholders – the owners (members of a society or majority shareholders in a company).

✗ Executive Management – the people responsible for the operations and results of the organisation, consisting of contributing partners or a board of directors.

✗ Customers – the individuals purchasing the design, these are often the end-users and the focal point of traditional design processes.

✗ Employees – all divisions of staff within an organisation across the spectrum of management to front-line staff.

✗ Suppliers – internal or external entities (e.g. a person or organisation) that provide a resource or service to the organisation.

✗ Community/Society – committees and other public groups that can influence the reputation of the organisation, product or service.

In any given design process, the designer is responsible for identifying the key stakeholder groups and their needs or requirements and is then tasked with balancing these to the best of their abilities. The principal tenet here is that stakeholders affect, and are affected by, an organisation and its decisions (Freeman, 1984). Naturally, a designer's consciousness of design practice (in its entirety) and their ability to manage it will influence on the final outcomes of the design – so it is important that these stakeholders (and their needs) are not overlooked. Failure to consider the stakeholders at the beginning of design can also lead to insurmountable barriers to implementation. For example, not properly engaging the employees and shareholders who will need to internally approve your project prior to its commencement may lead to delays, or failure to consult with a major regulatory body might lead to the final design output not being approved for launch.

We are not only concerned with stakeholders as a stage-gate for approval, as such a view would entirely overlook their value. A designer is also concerned with the intrinsic value of stakeholders in their relationship with an organisation's processes and outcomes (Jones & Wicks, 1999). Stakeholders represent a wealth of knowledge that can be tapped into when undertaking preliminary design work, which is why it is the core aspect of **CONSIDER**. Their continued engagement through the design process can not only ensure desirability but can also serve to ensure that the designer remains focused on the bigger picture rather than their own set of assumptions.

With all this in mind, the role of stakeholders in the design innovation process is quite clear. They present both the linchpins of design, as well as sense-makers and guides for our decision making. The two tools we present for **CONSIDER** are The Stakeholder Map and Organisational Conditions Framework. These can assist you to better understand your stakeholders and frame their needs.

The origin of **STAKEHOLDER MAPPING** can likely be traced back to environmental scanning. Its premise, as detailed by Mendelow (1981), is collecting information about an organisation's environment in order to reduce uncertainty. More recently, the model has been adapted to gauge the dynamics between the power and interests of an organisation's stakeholders (Johnson, Scholes, & Whittington, 2005). It has also been simplified, so that the user can identify the importance of different sets of stakeholders.

A stakeholder map allows us to visually map all the stakeholders for a given design project (whether you are designing a product, service, business model or another output of design). This is useful, as it can help you become cognisant of actors that you may have overlooked. It can also help you to recognise what groups you might need to engage with to make sure that your design is a success. These groups might include:

X CUSTOMERS OR USERS THAT CAN HELP YOU DETERMINE IF YOUR DESIGN IS HEADING IN THE RIGHT DIRECTION

X MEMBERS IN AN ORGANISATION THAT WILL ULTIMATELY CHOOSE WHETHER YOUR DESIGN CAN PROCEED (AND IF THE ORGANISATION WILL INVEST FURTHER RESOURCES IN IT)

X THE REGULATORY BODIES YOU MUST COMPLY WITH FOR YOUR DESIGN TO REACH THE MARKET.

Unlike other tools used by designers that might leave you with a tangible outcome, like the root cause of a problem or a value proposition, the outcomes of stakeholder map can feel quite intangible —simply 'identifying' a group of stakeholders doesn't really tell you what you need to be doing with them or how they should be engaged. Therefore, the key here is to remain conscious of the identified groups as you proceed with your design, and to regularly review how you can engage with them at critical junctures and key milestones.

The basic process of creating a stakeholder map is quite simple, and involves **BRAINSTORMING, SEGMENTING** and **PLANNING.** The following outline each step to help you start the process.

BRAINSTORM the various stakeholders for a given design. There are some basic stakeholders that you can always expect to see, like users and customers, but, when possible, try to avoid these in favour of more specific groups. For instance, you could frame your users as a persona (or set of personas) that you developed for that context, rather than using the generic term 'user', and refer to specific regulatory bodies. So again, focus on specifics.

SEGMENT. Now you're going to want to synthesise your list of stakeholders into something meaningful. This is going to require you to apply some of your own intuition and critical thinking, as there is no one correct way of segmenting stakeholders. There are three basic ways to segment:

1. thematically through groups (see below) where each type of stakeholder is linked through branches to the broader group that encompasses them (see the categories of stakeholders previously described)

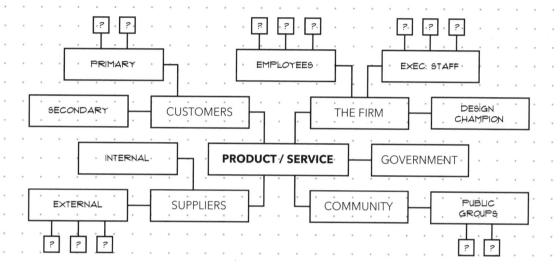

2. based on their level/degree of relationship (e.g. first [core/essential], second [direct/important] and third [indirect/interesting] degree stakeholders – as seen in example below)

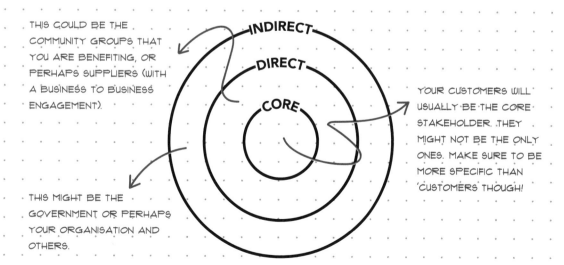

3. according to their level of interest and power (this is a power versus interest grid). This approach results in four categories of stakeholders (Bryson, 2003):

✗ Key Players – who have both an interest and significant power
✗ Subjects – who you need to keep informed as they have an interest, but little power
✗ Context setters – who should be kept satisfied as they have power, but little direct interest
✗ Crowd – consisting of stakeholders with little interest or power, therefore requiring minimal effort.

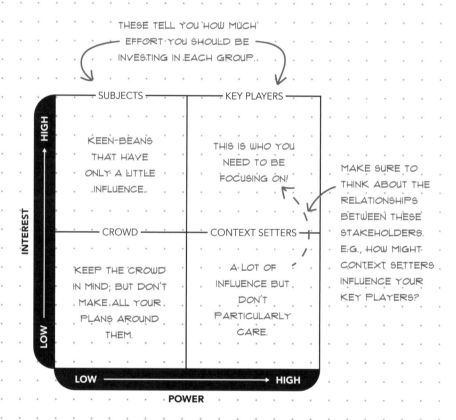

THESE TELL YOU 'HOW MUCH' EFFORT YOU SHOULD BE INVESTING IN EACH GROUP.

SUBJECTS — KEY PLAYERS

HIGH

KEEN-BEANS THAT HAVE ONLY A LITTLE INFLUENCE.

THIS IS WHO YOU NEED TO BE FOCUSING ON!

INTEREST

CROWD — CONTEXT SETTERS

KEEP THE CROWD IN MIND; BUT DON'T MAKE ALL YOUR PLANS AROUND THEM.

A LOT OF INFLUENCE BUT DON'T PARTICULARLY CARE.

LOW

LOW ——————→ HIGH

POWER

MAKE SURE TO THINK ABOUT THE RELATIONSHIPS BETWEEN THESE STAKEHOLDERS. E.G., HOW MIGHT CONTEXT SETTERS INFLUENCE YOUR KEY PLAYERS?

We recommend that you think critically about the purpose of your stakeholder map and determine your own method of categorisation or create a hybrid of these approaches. For example, you could first map stakeholders across their degree of engagement using three concentric circles, then split these circles across two axes that are determined based on the context of your design.

One axis could represent the split between internal (e.g. the designer, project manager, CEO, executive team, etc.) and external (e.g. the customer, user, regulatory bodies, etc.) stakeholders, and the other might help you differentiate between users and customers. You could also divide your circles into segments (like a pie chart), with each segment denoting one category of stakeholders that are then classified across their degree of engagement.

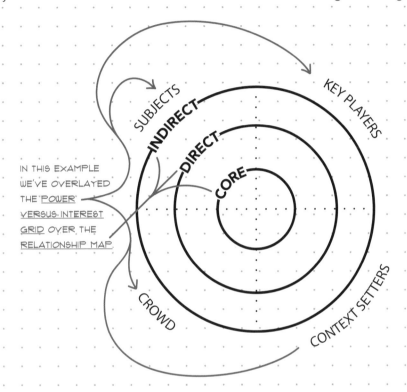

IN THIS EXAMPLE WE'VE OVERLAYED THE "POWER" VERSUS INTEREST GRID OVER THE RELATIONSHIP MAP.

PLAN. As mentioned before, identifying and segmenting your stakeholders is only the first part. Now you need to consider how to make this information useful. This might entail planning or listing the different types of ways to engage with each stakeholder group or determining how to better incorporate each group as part of the design process.

When we broke down the **CONSIDER** component, we discussed that context is comprised of:
1. ARCHAEOLOGY
2. THE ENTITY
3. THE ECOSYSTEM.

If you consider these three factors as a broader system or a shared mental model, then you can start to see the stakeholders that underline each of these factors. It is the collective beliefs, values and perceptions of stakeholders that form the foundation of context – so understanding stakeholders is an integral part of understanding context. A **STAKEHOLDER MAP** can help you to identify and segment the stakeholders for a given design, which is the first step to better understanding them (how can you understand something if you don't know what it is!).

Designers are known for being able to take a gestalt (holistic) view of a given context (Micheli, Wilner, Bhatti, Mura, & Beverland, 2019). As designers, it is no wonder that our thinking sometimes strays beyond the direct concerns of the project we are addressing. When doing this we are able to consider aspects that are not traditionally associated with design — aspects like innovation management, and the future and longevity of design in the context in which it is being practised. These concerns form the theoretical foundations of the **ORGANISATIONAL CONDITIONS FRAMEWORK**, which is further detailed later in this book the section **ORGANISATIONAL CONDITIONS**.

The organisational conditions framework is a tool for understanding:
× THE CURRENT STATE OF AN ORGANISATION IN RELATION TO THE DIRECTIVE(S) IT PROVIDES FOR DESIGN
× ITS STRATEGIC VISION FOR THE FUTURE OF THE ORGANISATION
× ITS CULTURAL CAPITAL AND CAPACITY AND WILLINGNESS TO ACTION DESIGN
× THE FACILITIES AND RESOURCES IT OFFERS TO ITS STAFF.

A designer, by considering these individual conditions for design, is able to determine the support (or lack of support) for design within an organisation. In turn, this allows the designer to grapple with potential barriers to practising design, or to increase the likelihood that a design project or concept is accepted. While this doesn't directly affect the output of design, it does help us to understand the entity in which design is being practised (which we have established is a core factor of the **CONSIDER** component). You can have the best concept in the world, but this is a moot point if the organisation isn't open to helping you get it off the ground. The organisational conditions can help the designer do homework on how much support they might garner and, more importantly, identify areas in which design could be better supported — so that these can be strategically built up alongside a design project.

The organisational conditions framework is split across strategic and operational aspects spanning:
× DIRECTIVE(S)
× STRATEGIC VISION
× CULTURAL CAPITAL
× FACILITIES.

The framework (on the next page) poses a series of questions across these dimensions to help guide the user to better understand and inquire about the current state of each of the conditions in an organisation. Answering the questions paints a broad picture of the current state of each of the conditions, which demonstrates whether they have been well considered and highlights both opportunities for improvement and what the organisation is currently doing well. Once identified, these opportunities can be used to build a case for improving the support for design in an organisation, or the designer can organically grow and develop the conditions.

STRATEGIC VISION

The overall vision and value proposition of an organisation—describing the organisation's strategic direction, it's appetite for change or innovation, and its risk aversion.

× DOES THE ORGANISATION HAVE A VISION FOR THE FUTURE (AN AIM OR MISSION)?
× DOES THE ORGANISATION HAVE APPETITE FOR CHANGE OR INNOVATION?

DIRECTIVE(S)

The organisation's directives which denote that the organisation's people are accountable in demonstrating and practicing design.

× ARE THE ORGANISATION'S PEOPLE HELD ACCOUNTABLE IN PRACTICING DESIGN?
× ARE THERE KEY PERFORMANCE INDICATORS WHICH DETAIL DESIGN PRACTICE?
× ARE THERE ROLES IN THE ORGANISATION WHICH REFLECT DESIGN PRACTICE?

FACILITIES

The organisation's facilities, referring to the extent to which it supports emerging design initiatives (with a focus on the physical environment and resources).

× IS DESIGN GIVEN A SPACE WITHIN THE ORGANISATION?
× ARE THE REQUIRED RESOURCES FOR DESIGN PROVIDED?

CULTURAL CAPITAL

The capacity of the organisation's people in practicing design—i.e. their knowledge of how to practice design and their understanding of the value it offers.

× DO THE ORGANISATION'S PEOPLE KNOW HOW TO PRACTICE DESIGN?
× DO THE ORGANISATION'S PEOPLE UNDERSTAND THE VALUE DESIGN OFFERS?

DRIVING QUESTIONS

CONSIDER

Why does your company, product or service exist?
✕ *What purpose does it serve?*

Describe the type of organisation you are in (the entity practicing design).
✕ *E.g., are you in a start-up, mature business, government body or other type of organisaiton?*
✕ *Are there any constraints in the context of your industry that you need to be aware of?*
✕ *Are there any laws, regulatory bodies, key social groups, etc. that need to be identified and considered?*

What can be learned from any legacy products (archaeology) or the company's existing solutions?
✕ *Are there any existing or legacy designs that will influence how a design is internally and externally perceived or adopted?*
✕ *Can these solutions determine the future direction and scope of your project?*
✕ *Are there any affordances and conventions that you need to be aware of?*

Who are the major stakeholders?
Describe your solution and/or organisational strategy.
✕ *Is everyone in the organisation aware of and in alignment with this strategy?*

Are there any unique considerations for the industry or sector your project is in?

Can you learn from any other industries or sectors that have addressed similar problems or opportunities well?

Does your design have the support (eco-system) it requires to function?

Are there any existing or legacy designs that will influence how a design is perceived and adopted inside the company?

What support does your design need and how could it be gained?

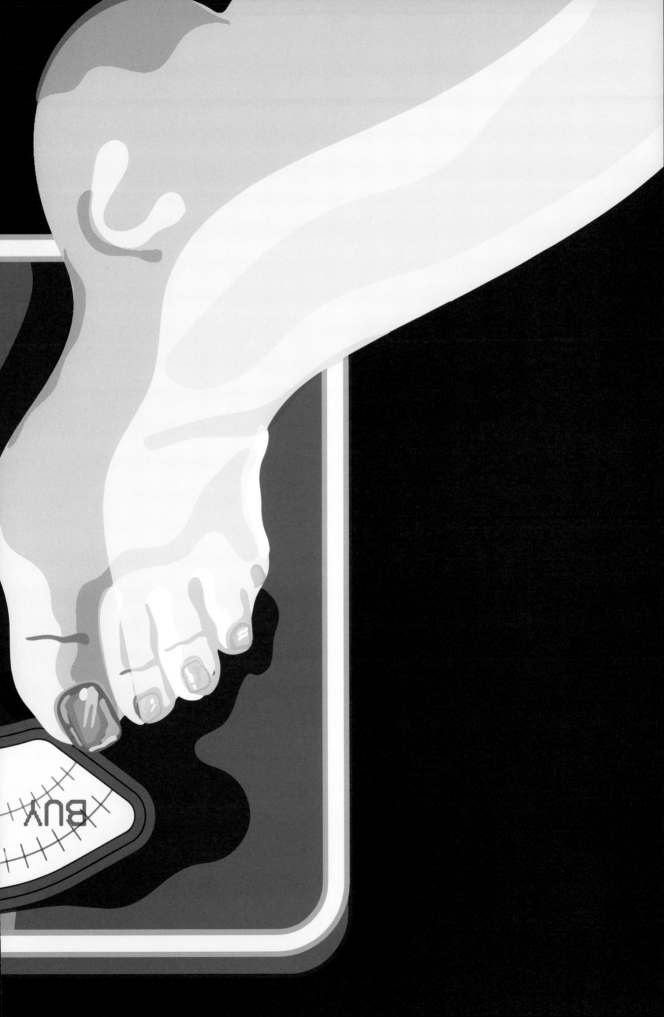

AUDIT

The first component, **CONSIDER**, was focused on understanding the context of design. **AUDIT** involves further inquiries into the context, with the aim of developing the designer's understanding of all relevant factors for design and acquiring insights. These insights are what will differentiate your design from others, ensure that stakeholders' needs are met, and are required for framing **INTENT** (the next component). Audits vary based on whether design has an internal focus (i.e. seeking to create change within an organisation) or external focus (i.e. seeking to create change outside of an organisation), and whether it's an intrapreneurial or entrepreneurial activity.

As we described earlier in the book, the key difference between design entrepreneurs and intrapreneurs is the focus of design. Most people understand the term entrepreneur as defined by Davidsson (2003), as 'the process of designing, launching and running a new business, which is often initially a small business'. Conversely, intrapreneurs seek to create change within an organisation, such as the design and launch of a new business model or an organisational restructure. Design audits spanning these two dimensions have fundamentally different focuses. Entrepreneurs might focus on market and user needs, while intrapreneurs might focus on assessing a particular capability (usually design) or practice within an organisation. Regardless of the focus, a plethora of methods exist to help with conducting an **AUDIT**, and these should be selected to correspond to the perspective of design (i.e. external vs. internal focus).

EXTERNAL

When design has an external focus, the audit is usually concerned with LATENT USER NEEDS, which generally inform the design of outputs like products and services or MARKET TRENDS, which can help to frame opportunities for business model innovation. The focus of your design will be the determining factor for selecting the best approach to use for the audit. Indeed, depending on its structure, an audit can assist in developing an understanding of market conditions, the current state of a product or service or the opportunities that exist within a given context (Nusem et al., 2020) – simply put, the audit can help you understand the current state of things. If you want to explore user needs, then this could be done by investigating the functions of existing designs, and then comparing these functions to users' needs. A discrepancy between the two would highlight user needs that are not being addressed, which could then help you frame your design intent. Similarly, you could investigate the business models that exist in your industry and compare the offerings to user needs. This could highlight any white space opportunities that have been overlooked by prevalent operational models.

Internal design audits are primarily undertaken to understand the outcomes of, and attitudes toward, design within an organisation (Cooper, Junginger, & Lockwood, 2013). Usually, such audits are structured to understand how a given capability works (or doesn't); thus informing a plan for maximising the potential of this given capability (Turner, 2013). A design audit with an internal focus reveals if there is design coherence in the way in which an organisation communicates its values and beliefs, and compares how an organisation operates and behaves internally (Best, 2015). They are not limited to analysis of the organisation itself, and sometimes require analysis of the organisation's environment. If you used the **ORGANISATIONAL CONDITIONS FRAMEWORK** in the last component, then you may already have some internal insights.

Generally speaking, there are two primary approaches for structuring audits.

1. Using secondary data that is publicly available.

2. Using primary data, which can be collected through qualitative methods

While the second approach is considered more difficult, insights which emerge from it can be much richer than those from secondary data.

Regardless of the focus of the audit and the approach selected, the primary function of an **AUDIT** is to discover insights that can be used to frame the intent of design and establish the desired outcomes of the design.

INTERNAL

CAN HELP THE USER BECOME MORE ACQUAINTED WITH AN INDUSTRY (AND IS THEREFORE SUITABLE FOR A NOVICE OR SOMEONE WHO IS EXPLORING A GIVEN INDUSTRY FOR THE FIRST TIME). IT ALSO REQUIRES VERY LIMITED RESOURCES.

CAN BE COLLECTED THROUGH QUALITATIVE METHODS LIKE SEMI-STRUCTURED INTERVIEWS OR FOCUS GROUPS.

COMPARATIVELY TIME CONSUMING AND COSTLY. + MORE COMPLEX

REQUIRES A PRIOR UNDERSTANDING OF THE DESIGN CONTEXT (THE INTERVIEWER MUST HAVE A MODICUM OF EXPERTISE WITH THE CONTEXT) AND HAS MORE SIGNIFICANT ETHICAL CONSIDERATIONS (DEPENDING ON THE INSTITUTE FROM WHICH DESIGN IS STEMMING) (NUSEM ET AL; 2020).

INSIGHTS

CORE INSIGHTS

The core aspect of **AUDIT** is to gain insights. Insights are gained in a process of continual questioning that leads to a greater understanding about a person, context or thing. It generally isn't driven or based on hard facts or evidence, but a feeling or emotion directed by your intuition. Part of the **AUDIT** process is analysis, which aims to understand a current, past or future context. An analysis of a single aspect may not in itself create unique insights, however, the evaluation of multiple aspects can. As discussed in **AUDIT**, insights can include both the internal and external environment of an organisation. Internal insight can include information about the business model, resources and capabilities of the company, while external insights can explore customer's behaviours, desires and needs (customer insights) and broader trends to identify gaps or opportunities in the market (market insights). We've talked a little bit about internal insights when going over CONSIDER (specifically when we talked about 'the entity practicing design' and the organisational conditions), so we are going to focus on external insights here.

MARKET INSIGHTS

As we see in David Attenborough's nature documentaries, the environment is what gives an animal their means of survival. The same goes for organisations. By understanding the environment, we are able to identify opportunities and threats, anticipate possible futures and even influence change. The macro environment includes factors that impact most organisations and should aim to identify how future issues across multiple realms might affect the organisation.

THESE INCLUDE:

✕ POLITICS
✕ ECONOMICS
✕ SOCIETY
✕ TECHNOLOGY
✕ ECOLOGY
✕ LAW

External insights can also include identifying key drivers of change in a specific industry or sector. We usually cluster an industry or sector through organisations (also known as competitors) that provide similar, if not the same, products or services. Every organisation has and always will have competitors. It is important to not scope your industry too narrowly, as using a wider lens for selecting competitors can give you a broader perspective, ensure you don't miss any potential threats of market entry, and help you identify 'white space' in the market (i.e., opportunities that haven't been capitalised on). You should aim to know as much as possible about your competition; as per the saying, 'keep your friends close but keep your enemies closer'.

A simple way to start is to Question, Identify and Evaluate. The following prompts can help you to start this process:

Question:
× WHAT INDUSTRY OR SECTOR DO WE BELONG TO?
× WHO ARE THE OTHER COMPANIES IN THIS INDUSTRY OR SECTOR?
× WHAT ARE OUR COMPANY RESOURCES (ASSETS, INTELLECTUAL PROPERTY, PEOPLE)?
× WHAT ARE OUR COMPANY'S CAPABILITIES?
× HOW ARE WE DIFFERENT FROM THE COMPETITION?

Identify:
× WHO DO WE DIRECTLY COMPETE WITH?
× WHO ARE OUR MOST INTENSE COMPETITORS? LESS INTENSE?
× CAN OUR COMPETITORS BE GROUPED INTO STRATEGIC GROUPS ON THE BASIS OF ASSETS, COMPETENCIES, OR STRATEGIES?
× WHO ARE POTENTIAL COMPETITIVE ENTRANTS? WHAT ARE THEIR BARRIERS TO ENTRY?

Evaluate:
× WHAT ARE THE COMPETITION'S OBJECTIVES AND STRATEGIES?
× DO THEY HAVE A MISSION AND VISION?
× OVER TIME WHAT COMPETITOR HAS BEEN THE MOST SUCCESSFUL/UNSUCCESSFUL? WHY?
× IS THERE ANY 'WHITE SPACE' IN THE INDUSTRY OR SECTOR, OR IS IT SATURATED?
× COULD ANY OF OUR COMPETITORS POTENTIALLY BE A COMPLEMENTOR (PROVIDE AN OPPORTUNITY FOR COOPERATION)?

Throughout history there have been many 'game changers' to most markets. On page 204* we have included a challenging activity to get you thinking about major disruptors to several different industries. There is no limitation of the era or type of disruption you choose, as long as you can provide an explanation for it.

Throughout history there have been many 'game changers' to most markets. We have included **MARKET DISRUPTORS** template, a challenging activity to get you thinking about major disruptors to several different industries. There is no limitation of the era or type of disruption you choose, as long as you can provide an explanation for it.

CUSTOMER INSIGHTS

These types of insights provide a deeper understanding of the behaviours, desires and needs of customers. Such insights can be uncovered through existing customers or potential future customers. The methods for gaining customer insights are primarily qualitative in nature and commonly used in ethnographic research.

Customer insights build upon Verganti's (2006) proposition of user push (understanding customer needs), rather than market pull (making decisions-based market requirements). Customer insights require questioning beyond superficial needs and satisfaction to understand what a customer values. 'Value' is usually not related to a product, it is connected to an individual's cultural and educational background; financial position and life experiences. The process should not only question a person's current situation but also aim to anticipate any future desires, needs or goals. Like all qualitative approaches, or design methods in general, they are not straightforward, and we cannot offer set rules to follow.

EXAMPLES INCLUDE:

✕ INTERVIEWS
✕ CUSTOMER
   PERSONAS
✕ STORYTELLING +
   NARRATIVES
✕ SCENARIOS
✕ OBSERVATIONS
✕ SHADOWING.

A simple way to start is to Identify, Examine, and Absorb. The following prompts can help guide you through this process:

Identify (customers or users):
✕ WHO USES OR WILL USE THE SOLUTION?
✕ ARE THE CUSTOMERS ALSO THE USERS? IS THE SAME PERSON PAYING AND USING THE DESIGN?
✕ WHO BENEFITS THE MOST? WHO WOULD LOSE?

Examine (personal assumptions):
✕ WHAT DO YOU EXPECT YOUR CUSTOMERS' DESIRES AND NEEDS TO BE?
✕ WHAT EXPERIENCES HAVE LED YOU TO THINK YOUR SOLUTION IS THE BEST ONE FOR THE CUSTOMER?
✕ HOW CERTAIN ARE YOU THAT YOU ARE CORRECT?

Absorb (ask questions):

× WHAT ARE THE CUSTOMER'S BELIEFS, NEEDS AND DESIRES?

× HOW DO THE CUSTOMER'S BELIEFS, NEEDS AND DESIRES EXPLAIN THEIR PROBLEM?

× WHAT IS THE REASON FOR THE PROBLEM OR OPPORTUNITY YOU ARE EXPLORING?

People, organisations, and environments are complex. The process of gaining an insight therefore should not be anticipated to be simple. It, once again, comes down to your abilities as a designer to follow your intuition. Insights are subtle and usually a time-consuming task to acquire. Interpreting qualitative data and discerning valid insights requires expertise. Therefore, to start learning this process, the two tools we present for **AUDIT** are **BUSINESS MODEL CONTENT ANALYSIS** and **CUSTOMER SEGMENT PROFILES**. One way of deriving insights is to synthesise the findings from research on an organisation's market and customers, and to identify patterns between these two areas. This can reveal opportunities to create new value for customers and the organisation. Keep in mind that great inspiration can come from looking outside the defined area or scope of a project.

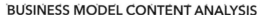

BUSINESS MODEL CONTENT ANALYSIS

As a starting point watch a few YouTube videos on business models, or better still read The Business Model Generation: A Handbook for Visionaries, Game Changers, and Challengers by Osterwalder and Pigneur (2010). This will give you the background you need to complete a business model canvas. We use the canvas to not only design and prototype different business models, but also to analyse different companies in a selected industry for evaluation and comparison. It is this second type of use that is appropriate for an audit. Through this process you will be able to synthesise knowledge gained from real companies to identify opportunities in the market, industry and/or sector. Analysing companies on their business model can help reveal opportunities for innovation that may not be uncovered through analysing product or service offerings.

When conducting a business model content analysis, you should first make a list of all your competitors. Once you have captured all of your competitors (or at least the ones you can think of), select a manageable number (~10–20). Your selection should be guided by trying to achieve a representative sample of the types of organisations in your sector. For each company, write the name of the company in the first column, then continue to fill in the remaining columns:

COMPANY SIZE & LOCATION/S: the number of employees, stores or headquarters and the location i.e. continent, country, region, state, city or suburb.

TYPE OF COMPANY: non-for-profit, start-up, multinational

VALUE PROPOSITION: a statement summarising the customer problems being solved and the customer needs being satisfied

CORE VALUES: the principles and beliefs that are important to the organisation

OFFERINGS: the organisation's suite of products and services provided to their customers

REVENUE STREAMS: this is how the company makes money, could be through one time purchase or a subscription model for example.

CHANNELS: this is the way they distribute, communicate and reach customers. It should include both digital and physical channels.

CUSTOMER RELATIONSHIP/S: this explains how they wish to engage with customer segments, could be purely transactional or something that aims to create a long-term engagement.

RESOURCES: this includes all the assets that the company has (this could be human, technology, intellectual property or property assets).

PARTNERSHIPS: this a network of companies, suppliers or organisations which help the company operate

DISTINGUISHING FACTOR: this is a key feature that makes a company appealing to a customer segment.

To find this data start with a Google search on each company. Continue to explore multiple sources to find the information that is required. The more information you can find and include the better your insights will be. The insight might be understanding what the company's distinguishing factor or competitive advantage is. If this process does not yield any insights, **BUSINESS MODEL SWOT** has been included to provide another level of analysis by promoting you to explore the Strengths, Weaknesses, Opportunities and Threats of each of your competitors. The last step in this process is to add your own company to the sheet. You can then use the information collected to **PLOT THE COMPETITION**. It is a simple matrix to represent the relationships between an organisation's proposed market position to its competitors, allowing for comparison and opportunities in the market to be highlighted.

WHERE CAN YOU FIND INFORMATION?

- ✕ DIGITAL CHANNELS: E.G WEBSITES, MOBILE APPLICATIONS
- ✕ ANNUAL REPORTS
- ✕ FINANCIAL REPORTS
- ✕ SERVICE BROCHURES
- ✕ INFORMATION SHEETS
- ✕ MEDIA RELEASES
- ✕ MEDIA COVERAGE (NEWS ARTICLES; TELEVISION REPORTS)
- ✕ MARKET ANALYSIS
- ✕ RESEARCH REPORTS
- ✕ INTERVIEWS

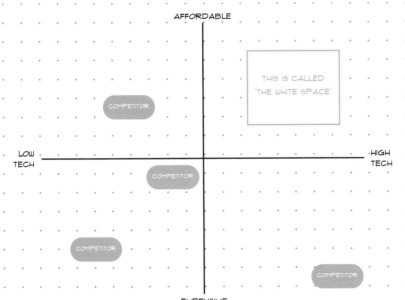

PLOT THE COMPETITION!

SO SIMPLE, YET SO USEFUL

✕ ONCE YOU HAVE DONE A COMPETITOR ANALYSIS ON YOUR COMPETITION

✕ DRAW A MATRIX (OR USE THE TEMPLATE AT THE BACK)

✕ GIVE EACH AXIS A NAME THIS SHOULD BE A SHORT DESCRIPTION OF WHAT IS CURRENTLY AVAILABLE ON THE MARKET

✕ WRITE THE NAME OR PLACE THE LOGO OF EACH COMPETITOR ON THE MATRIX

✕ YOU WANT TO YOUR COMPANY TO BE IN THE TOP RIGHT HAND CORNER

BUSINESS MODEL ANALYSIS EXAMPLE

The following is an example of a business model analysis of a selection of fitness companies. The template included in the back of the book is completely blank so you can add your own heading. A list of possible things to include in your analysis are outlined on the previous page. Aim to include as much information as you can!

INCLUDE YOUR
COMPANY!
HOW DO
YOU COMPARE?

NUMBER OF
EMPLOYEES

COMPANY NAME	VALUE PROPOSITION	COMPANY SIZE
GYM 24/7	PROVIDING YOU ACCESS TO FITNESS WHEN YOU WANT IT	10,000+
GOODTIME GYM	CONNECTING YOUNG PEOPLE WITH GOOD HEALTH ROUTINES	1,000-5,000
BREAK HILL GYM	HIGH QUALITY EQUIPMENT WITH HIGH QUALITY TRAINERS	<30
FITNESS HUB	LIFE-LONG FITNESS	1,000-5,000
UGYM	AFORDABLE FITNESS THAT SUITS YOUR NEEDS	200-500
FITNESS WORLD	UNIQUE WAYS OF GETTING FIT SO YOU LIVE A LONGER + HEALTHIER LIFE	10,000+
TONE TIME	CUTTING THE COSTS OF PERSONAL TRAINING	1,000-5,000
TRUE FITNESS	CREATING A FITNESS COMMUNITY	<50

USUALLY FOUND ON THEIR WEBSITE
OR MARKETING MATERIAL YOU CAN
CREATE ONE WHICH EMBODIES THE COMPANY.

TOP TIP: START WITH THEIR WEBSITE, AND IF AVAILABLE DOWNLOAD ANNUAL REVIEWS.

INCLUDE BOTH
PHYSICAL + DIGITAL

EXPLAINED ON
THE NEXT PAGE

LOCATION	CHANNELS	CUSTOMER SEGMENT
INTERNATIONAL	MULTIPLE GYMS FACEBOOK PAGE WEBSITE MOBILE APP	YOUNG & SERIOUS
NATIONAL	GYMS WEBSITE	YOUNG & SERIOUS
LOCAL	ONE GYM INSTAGRAM WEBSITE	YOUNG & SERIOUS
NATIONAL	GYM IN MAIN CITIES WEBSITE	AGELESS FITNESS
NATIONAL	GYMS MOBILE APP	YOUNG & SERIOUS
INTERNATIONAL	GYMS MOBILE APP ALL SOCIAL MEDIA	FITNESS ENTHUSIASTS
NATIONAL	GYMS WEBSITE	FITNESS ENTHUSIASTS
LOCAL	GYM WEBSITE	LIFE-LONG FITNESS

FINDING PATTERNS IN THE DATA

WHAT MAKES
COMPANIES SIMILAR?

CUSTOMER SEGMENTATION is the first step in defining and selecting a target market to pursue and involves splitting an overall market into two or more groups of customers. Each individual group (or market segment) should denote a typology of customers based on archetypal characteristics or product needs. There are multiple reasons to segment like this:

✕ TO IDENTIFY AND UNDERSTAND POTENTIAL MARKETS TO ENTER

✕ TO UNDERSTAND YOUR COMPETITIVE POSITIONING, AS IT CAN SOMETIMES BE EASIER TO COMPETE BY FOCUSING ON A SMALLER, MORE DEFINED GROUP OF CUSTOMERS

✕ TO PROVIDE NEW OPPORTUNITIES; BY BEING CREATIVE IN THE WAY IN WHICH YOU SEGMENT A MARKET, YOU COULD GENERATE NEW INSIGHTS INTO POTENTIAL AREAS TO EXPLORE.

It can be easy to segment a market based on products, rather than the customer (when it is a product it is usually referred to as a sub-market). Traditionally markets are segmented by:

GEOGRAPHY, when you separate customers based on where they are. This could be done at any scale: continent, country, region, state, city or suburb.

DEMOGRAPHY, which is the most popular due to it being the easiest and more reliable process, including basic information about a person, including:
✕ AGE
✕ GENDER
✕ INCOME
✕ EDUCATION
✕ FAMILY
✕ LIFE STAGE
✕ OCCUPATION.

PSYCHOGRAPHY, in a mix of other types of segmentation, like age or religion (demographic) or their location (geographic), but explores:
✕ LIFESTYLE
✕ INTERESTS
✕ OPINIONS
✕ CONCERNS
✕ PERSONALITY
✕ VALUES
✕ ATTITUDES.

BEHAVIOUR, largely related to a person's buying behaviours, including how they make decisions: are they loyal or benefit seeking (e.g. variety, price, or maximum value)?

When thinking about your customer segment, you may want to explore all or a combination of different aspects. Another approach is to start with selecting a market, identifying sub-markets, and then creating market segments using the information above. The template, **SEGMENTING CUSTOMERS** is included for you to explore how to do this. Existing market research data can also be analysed to identify patterns of recurring goals, behaviours and attitudes to form customer segments. Once a customer segment has been identified, a profile for them can be created. Similar to a persona, a market segment profile expands to include information on the market rather than just a person. The process can also be conducted on products (see **PRODUCT ANALYSIS** template).

When you start segmenting customers, give each segment a catchy name. Not only is this fun but it helps explain the difference between groups. It is also useful as you can quickly identify and understand the different segments when they are discussed in reports, presentations and meetings.

SOME EXAMPLES OF MARKET SEGMENT NICKNAMES:
- X COST CONSCIOUS
- X QUALITY FOCUSED
- X HEALTH CONSCIOUS
- X BRAND CONSCIOUS
- X ENVIRONMENTALLY AWARE
- X CONVENIENCE DRIVEN
- X RELATIONSHIP FOCUSED
- X VARIETY SEEKERS
- X CASUAL BUYERS
- X 'DO IT YOURSELF'
- X COMFORT DRIVEN

A WELL-KNOWN EXAMPLE OF A NICKNAME IS 'BABY BOOMERS', WHICH REFERS TO THE GENERATION OF PEOPLE BORN AFTER 1945 UP UNTIL THE EARLY 1960S.

CUSTOMER SEGMENT PROFILE EXAMPLE

The following is an example of a customer segment profile. The customer segment is called "Young & Serious" and is a customer group from the fitness industry (previous tool). The main sections can be found on the template at the back of the book. This example provides you an example of what you should be including and key questions to ask yourself for each section.

INDUSTRY: FITNESS   **SEGMENT NICKNAME:** YOUNG & SERIOUS

SEGMENT SIZE MEASURES

ESTIMATED AT AROUND 10,000,000 PEOPLE ACROSS THE COUNTRY

HOW MANY PEOPLE ARE THERE IN THE SELECTED INDUSTRY?

PROPORTION OF THE OVERALL MARKET

WHAT PERCENTAGE/NUMBER OF PEOPLE REPRESENT THE CHOSEN MARKET SEGMENT?

10% OF ALL CONSUMERS

MAIN CONSUMER NEEDS

WANT TO GET INTO GREAT PHYSICAL SHAPE. LOOKING FOR STATE-OF-THE-ART FACILITIES, CONVENIENTLY LOCATED, LIKE TO MIX WITH OTHER PATRONS

WHAT IS THE KEY THINGS THIS CUSTOMER SEGMENT NEEDS?

USAGE LEVEL

HOW OFTEN DO THE USE THE PRODUCT OR SERVICE ON OFFER?

HIGH PROPORTION OF HEAVY USERS - GO TO A FITNESS CENTER SEVERAL TIMES A WEEK

LEVEL OF BRAND LOYALTY

HIGH LEVEL OF SWITCHING BEHAVIOR OVER TIME, MAY TRIAL A NEW FITNESS CENTER EVERY 1-2 YEARS, DUE TO INFLUENCE OF FRIENDS OR FOR SOMETHING DIFFERENT

HOW LOYAL IS THIS CUSTOMER SEGMENT TO A CHOSEN COMPANY OR BRAND?

PRICE SENSITIVITY

HOW IMPORTANT IS PRICE FOR THIS CUSTOMER SEGMENT?

PRICE IS A REASONABLY IMPORTANT FACTOR & DIFFERENT PRICE DEALS ARE IMPORTANT

RETAILER PREFERENCES

LIKES WELL-KNOWN CHAINS WITH MULTIPLE OUTLETS THAT HAVE CONVENIENT LOCATIONS

WHAT DOES THE CUSTOMER SEGMENT LOOK FOR IN A COMPANY/RETAILER?

PRODUCT INVOLVEMENT LEVELS

LOW-MEDIUM, AS THEY OFTEN SWITCH/TRIAL NEW FACILITIES THEY SPEND LESS TIME ON THE PRODUCT DECISION PROCESS

HOW INVOLVED ARE THEY IN THE PRODUCT/SERVICE?

GEOGRAPHIC SPREAD

FAIRLY WIDESPREAD, BUT THE HEAVIEST USERS IN THIS SEGMENT TEND TO LIVE OR WORK IN BUSY CITIES

DEMOGRAPHIC DESCRIPTION

YOUNGER (AGED 18 TO 30 YEARS), WELL EDUCATED, USUALLY EMPLOYED IN OFFICE OR SKILLED WORK, UPWARDLY MOBILE, SINGLE OR IN A RELATIONSHIP

PSYCHOGRAPHIC DESCRIPTION

QUITE SOCIAL, TRAVEL GOALS, ENJOY SPORT, ENVIRONMENTALLY CONCERNED, FOCUSED ON FUTURE GOALS & SUCCESS

AS EXPLAINED ON THE PREVIOUS PAGE

THIS IS INMPORTANT!
WHAT DO COMPANIES ON THE INDUSTRY CURRENTLY OFFER THIS CUSTOMER SEGMENT?

MAIN MEDIA CHOICES

- ✗ BIG USERS OF INTERNET
- ✗ MAJOR CONSUMERS OF REALITY TV SHOWS
- ✗ ACTIVE USERS OF SOCIAL MEDIA
- ✗ MORE LIKELY TO ENGAGE WITH MOBILE PHONE MARKETING

WHAT MEDIA DOES THE CUSTOMER SEGMENT USE?

MAIN COMPETITIVE OFFERINGS

- ✗ LARGE FITNESS CENTER CHAINS HEAVILY TARGET THIS SEGMENT
- ✗ SPECIALIST GYMS PREDOMINATELY TARGET THEM AS WELL
- ✗ GROWING NUMBER OF BOOT CAMP, STYLE FITNESS OFFERINGS
- ✗ VARIOUS SPORTS SHOULD BE CONSIDERED INDIRECT COMPETITORS

DRIVING
QUESTIONS

AUDIT

What is your competitive advantage?
✗ *What is it that differentiates you from your competitors?*
✗ *What is your current level of support for design within the business?*

What do your competitors' business models look like and how are you different?
✗ *What are the differences between you and your competitors' activities, partners, channels, value propositions, customer relationships and financial structures?*

What is the biggest threat to your market currently and in the future?
✗ *Is it a competitor, or driven by technology (e.g. artificial intelligence or machine learning)?*
✗ *What are some market trends that could be a force of disruption?*

Describe your customers and stakeholders:
✗ *Who are they?*
✗ *Why have they chosen to engage with your business, products and/or services?*
✗ *How can you segment them into different groups?*

What are the biggest issues your customers face in their daily lives?
✗ *Do your current offerings help address these?*

What do your customers value, need and want?
✗ *How do you address any or all of these?*
✗ *How does your strategy align with your customers' needs, wants and desires?*
✗ *Are you providing a solution to their key/daily problems?*

How do you currently engage with your customer?
✗ *What are your customers' aspirations, routines, and pain- and gain-points?*
✗ *What objectives do they have that your company can assist with?*

INTENT

INTENT helps us to define what value we are seeking to create, and for whom. This component will help you to frame the outcomes your design will endeavour to create, and these outcomes should correspond to insights that you have uncovered, presumably through your **AUDIT**. Intent that is not grounded by an insight is likely to lead you down the wrong path. There are three primary ways to frame intent, as:

1. an aim for design
2. an internal guide
3. a mission statement.

Design is the process of developing information about a specific situation that has not previously existed. The two previous components have created large amounts of new information. In order to inform intent, information must be collected (as explored in the previous two components) and synthesised through:

× DOCUMENTATION
× EXPLANATION
× MODIFICATION
× VERIFICATION
× ANALYSIS
× EXPLANATION
× IMPLEMENTATION.

Having a clear intent is critical for the successful translation of design outcomes and is dependent on having an accurate definition of the problem, and an understanding of the metrics of success (discussed further in **EVALUATE**). This stage is not about determining what the design itself should be, but rather establishing what the outcomes of design should be prior to designing. It's about understanding what the design aims to accomplish, and understanding the process required to make it happen.

A good statement of intent is:
× Concise and clear. It doesn't take long to get your head across or require a degree in rocket science to understand.
× Infers the problem addressed. It should infer what context we're looking at, is it education or fast fashion?
× Open, but not too open. Breadth means your potential design solution isn't locked in (good!), but too few constraints can have adverse effects on design.

Intent is the continuation of capturing and managing the information developed during the project.

Intent also serves as a record of the project that can be reviewed retrospectively to understand where it succeeded and why it failed in other areas – imagine it as your guiding light.

The 'users' of design intent can be separated into three groups:

1. DESIGNERS Typically, designers do not clearly remember why they made earlier design decisions and forget outstanding issues (Ullman, Dietterich, Stauffer, 1988). To mitigate this, design intent could be in the form of a notebook used to document the designer's design practice in a manner that is easily recovered. It can clarify the relationship between the information and determine the best path forward (Ensici, Badke-Schaub, Bayazit, Lauche, 2013).

2. THE PROJECT TEAM Intent can be used to ensure the project team are aware and confident of the design process. Projects are generally undertaken by a group of people, and a recorded history of decisions made is easily reviewed and used by team members and management to understand the state of the project. Regular meetings and presentations should be provided to ensure all group members are aware of new directions and decisions made.

3. PROJECT MANAGERS AND WIDER THE ORGANISATION. To keep abreast of the project progress, project managers should also be involved in this process. Clear intent supports communication with other levels in the organisation (often required for project support during the IMPLEMENTATION of a solution). People who are not a part of the project team should also be able to easily discern what was discussed, not just the final decision. This can be achieved by giving the project and the team a separate space or room in the organisation, where all employees can walk in and ask questions.

Framing your goals, aims, and the outcomes you wish to create through a strong intent will serve as a reminder of what you are trying to accomplish through design, and ensure that your decisions and progress remain aligned to these.

TYPES OF INFORMATION INCLUDED IN INTENT:

X PROBLEMS AND ISSUES ADDRESSED: BUSINESS ISSUES, ARTEFACT DESIGN ISSUES

X AREAS OF STRATEGIC IMPORTANCE/ OPPORTUNITY

X RESEARCH ON TRENDS, GAPS IN THE MARKETPLACE

X OPPORTUNITIES THAT HAVE BEEN IDENTIFIED (WITHOUT ANY HINT OF A SOLUTION OR WHAT FORMAT THE SOLUTION TAKES, E.G. A MOBILE APPLICATION OR PRODUCT)

X ALTERNATIVES CONSIDERED: TASKS, FUNCTIONS, FEATURES

X ARGUMENTS FOR AND AGAINST ALTERNATIVES: QUALITATIVE DISCUSSIONS, QUANTITATIVE ANALYSIS

X METHODS USED TO EVALUATE ALTERNATIVES

X CONSTRAINTS AND REQUIREMENTS

X ASSUMPTIONS MADE

X DECISION HISTORY AND RATIONALE FOR EACH DECISION.

VALUES

CORE **VALUE**

The core aspect of **INTENT** is value. As with many terms in the field of design, the term 'value' is plagued by terminological confusion. This is not surprising, given that the word is quite polysemous (Boztepe, 2007). When speaking of value, you could, for instance, be referring to:

✗ the economic return of a product or service
✗ the regard or importance of something
✗ standards of behaviour or what is important in life
✗ a set of principles or standards.

This spectrum of options presents a simple question: when we talk about value, what exactly do we mean?

It is important to start by first establishing that as individuals or organisations, we each have our own sets of values. As a designer, understanding these values is a core tenet – as without such an understanding we can't hope to design something that will be of real meaning (or value!) to stakeholders. So, when we talk about value, we are trying to establish how we could make the current state for a user, customer, or organisation better. In terms of aligning this to **INTENT**, you could frame this objective as better understanding the outcomes that would be valued by the stakeholders (in the sense of, e.g., quality of life, or social or economic aspects).

In practice this theory is generally translated to a value proposition – a statement that communicates an organisation's purpose, goals, motivations and/or beliefs with its stakeholders (Osterwalder & Pigneur, 2010). This seems simple but is surprisingly challenging. You see, when you ask an organisation what their values are (commonly referred to as an organisation's 'why'), more often than not we are presented with silence or with a range of diverse, sometimes radically different responses. It is hard for an organisation to identify why it does what it does as this is formed by a mix of culture, experience, meaning, values – a shared understanding that informs decisions and communications (Sinek, 2009). As designers, we are trained to think abductively, and to blend rationality and intuition (Micheli, Perks, & Beverland, 2018). These skills place us in an ideal position to pragmatically explore these fuzzy dimensions and grapple with concepts like 'value'.

Designers, in a more tangible sense, also explore the value of products, services, and other solutions that emerge from design practice. For such instances, value can be framed according to the goals that design helps the stakeholder to accomplish; or, again as described under **INTENT**, as the outcomes we are trying to achieve through the design of solutions. These two frames we describe – an organisation's why and stakeholders' goals – represent the primary ways that designers view and deal with value. In the next sections we outline two tools, **VALUE DEFINITION**; which can be used to help a designer frame an organisation's why and stakeholders' goals respectively; and a **DESIGN BRIEF**, which can help frame what the outcomes of a design should from a customer perspective.

VALUE DEFINITION

In his famous TED talk Simon Sinek (2009) introduced the 'Golden Circle' concept, which premises that people buy the why behind what you do, rather than what you do. The concept is comprised of three layers:

× WHY, which relates to why individuals pursue goals

× HOW, which refers to how these goals are achieved

× WHAT, which focuses on what these goals are

The following example of the much known company UBER, illustrates the differences between the three layers.

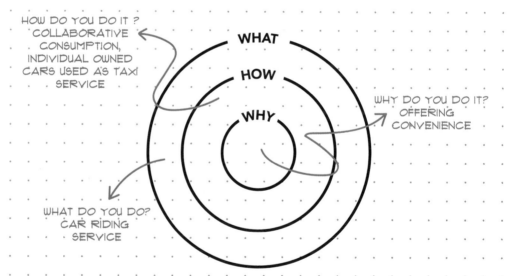

UBER – THE SMARTEST WAY TO GET AROUND

HOW DO YOU DO IT?
COLLABORATIVE
CONSUMPTION,
INDIVIDUAL OWNED
CARS USED AS TAXI
SERVICE

WHY DO YOU DO IT?
OFFERING
CONVENIENCE

WHAT DO YOU DO?
CAR RIDING
SERVICE

In organisations, this why can be communicated through a value proposition – which we previously covered as capturing an organisation's purpose, goals, motivations, and beliefs with its stakeholders. The core doctrine of the golden circle concept is that starting with one's why, rather than their what, is a significantly more compelling way of framing purpose. Many organisations find this process to be intangible and 'fluffy.' (Straker & Nusem, 2019), which is why we have provided a structured approach for this undertaking.

The value definition tool has been designed to, as can be expected by the name, help organisations define the value that they deliver to customers, and to frame how this 'value' can be aligned to customers' needs and ultimately improved. In realising this ambition, the tool reframes the doctrine of the golden circle concept through two distinct perspectives: the organisation's and its customers'. Unpacking the organisation's purpose through its internal perspective helps us to establish the current state, and to understand whether the organisation is comfortable grappling with concepts as vague as 'value'. Framing the organisation's why through its customers' perspectives then challenges the organisation to consider how it is perceived by its customers, which in turn helps it frame a new and compelling value proposition – one that is aligned to its customers' interests.

The value definition tool can help an organisation understand its why, and to frame a new and compelling why in the form of a value proposition. A value proposition is just one way of framing intent as, by definition, it helps to articulate the value an organisation seeks to offer its stakeholders – which is implicit in the outcomes that it hopes to produce.

The value definition tool is segmented across a horizontal and vertical dimension: A horizonal split places the organisation's perspective on the left-hand side and its customers' perspectives on the right. A vertical dimension then segments questions by their point of origin; i.e. outside-in (what, how, and why) depicting questions 1–3 at the top; and inside-out (why, how, and what) depicting questions 4–6 at the bottom (Straker & Nusem, 2019). To complete the framework the user simply follows the prompts:

VALUE DEFINITION EXAMPLE

Graceful Ageing is one of Australia's largest and oldest aged care organisation. After many decades of sucess they are now seeking assistance to innovate for growth in a dynamic environment, with emerging challenges driven by an ageing population and government reform initiatives. They know they need to innovate their value proposition to successful compete but also ensure they are meeting the next generation's aged care requirements.

1) WHAT DOES YOUR ORGANISATION DO?

x. PROVIDE HOME CARE, RETIREMENT LIVING AND RESIDENTIAL CARE SERVICES FOR THE ELDERLY.

CHANGE IN COMPANY STRATEGY IN 2020

2) HOW DOES YOUR ORGANISATION PERFORM ITS KEY ACTIVITIES?

PROVISION OF AGED CARE SERVICES THROUGH GOVERNMENT-SUBSIDISED PACKAGES.

3) WHY DOES YOUR ORGANISATION PERFORM THESE ACTIVITIES?

TO PROMOTE WELLBEING AND INDEPENDENCE FOR OUR FELLOW AUSTRALIANS.

4) WHY DOES THE ORGANISATION DO WHAT IT DOES?

TO REDEFINE THE EXPERIENCE OF AGEING AND GUIDE PEOPLE TO MAKE THE MOST OUT OF LIFE

5) HOW DOES THE ORGANISATION ACHIEVE THIS?

THROUGH PROACTIVE SERVICES—ENCOMPASSING BEHAVIOURAL CHANGE DRIVEN THROUGH GUIDANCE, MOTIVATION AND CONNECTION—WHICH IMPROVE AUSTRALIAN'S HEALTHY LIFE EXPECTANCY

6) WHAT CHANGES DOES THE ORGANISATION NEED TO DO TO REINFORCE THE WHY?

A REASON FOR ELDERLY AUSTRALIANS TO HAVE PURPOSE AND BE PRODUCTIVE IN THEIR LATER YEARS.

RE-DEFINE AGEING!

GRACEFUL AGEING

PROMOTE WELLBEING & INDEPENDENCE ✗
FOR OUR FELLOW AUSTRALIANS

THE COMPANY
MISSION
STATEMENT

1) WHAT DOES YOUR CUSTOMER THINK THE ORGANISATION DOES?

PROVIDE AGED CARE SERVICES FOR THE ELDERLY.

2) HOW DOES YOUR CUSTOMER THINK THE ORGANISATION PERFORMS ITS KEY ACTIVITIES?

THROUGH A RANGE OF SERVICES WHICH SUPPORT THE ELDERLY
IN THEIR HOMES AND IN THE ORGANISATION'S FACILITIES.

3) WHY DOES YOUR CUSTOMER CHOOSE YOU OVER YOUR COMPETITOR(S)?

BECAUSE THE ORGANISATION IS A NON-PROFIT WITH A SOCIAL
MISSION

4) WHY VALUE DO YOU PROVIDE TO YOUR CUSTOMER?

STAFF, THE LOCATION OF INFRASTRUCTURE (RESIDENTIAL CARE
ETC.), AND THE STATE OF THE INFRASTRUCTURE. ✗

NOT SURE
NEED TO DO
CUSTOMER
INTERVIEWS

5) HOW DOES YOUR CUSTOMER KNOW ABOUT THIS VALUE?

THROUGH PERSONALISED CARE AND SUPPORT.

6) WHAT CHANGES ARE NEEDED SO YOUR CUSTOMER KNOWS YOUR VALUE?

DEMONSTRATE AND COMMUNICATE THAT THE ORGANISATION IS
MORE THAN JUST AN AGED CARE PROVIDER, AND THAT IT IS
SEEKING TO REDEFINE THE EXPERIENCE OF AGEING.

A **DESIGN BRIEF** is a living document produced for a project team derived from the client or customer frame and viewpoint. A brief outlines the project scope and the necessary deliverables required to satisfy the stated customer goals. It is, according to Owen (1979), the most effective instrument for assisting a team to progress a design project with full confidence and expertise. They are used to not only inform design practice but also to determine and evaluate the deliverables of the project. The design brief can and will change over time, periodically adjusted to address any changes in the scope of the project. The design brief serves as a focal point that anchors the customer, the project team and the design team to a common "drill sheet" (the marching orders everyone plays to).

The design brief usually includes, but is not limited to, a company profile, problem description, constraints, costs, manufacturing possibilities, timeline, budget, goals, outcomes and deliverables. These design briefs also help you frame the outcomes of a design from a customer's perspective. A design brief plays a key role functioning as an effective means to ensure both high standards of design, and to reduce the time that the client spends in negotiations prior to project sign off.

The intrinsic value placed on the customers' perception, Customer Value, has become a key design driver. One prominent tool for measuring this is the Value Proposition Canvas (VPC) by Osterwalder, Pigneur, Bernarda and Smith (2014). . The VPC can assist you to map a product or service to what a customer values and needs, thus assisting in an alignment between product and market. The VPC is an example of an exemplary tool in the designer's quiver that can baseline and inform the **DESIGN BRIEF**.

The purpose of this method is to link insights **(AUDIT)** and the design of feasible solutions. From all the information gathered, you should begin to answer:

✕ HOW WOULD YOU FRAME THIS INTO A DESIGN INTENT?

✕ HOW COULD YOU BRIEF SOMEONE ON THE DIRECTION YOU WANT THE DESIGNERS TO GO TO ACHIEVE THE INTENDED OUTCOME?

Using the tool **DESIGN BRIEF**, map out the problems and the aspirations when solving that problem in as much detail as possible (use direct quotes if you have them), from the customer's perspective. The problems and aspirations fall into three broad categories – functional, social and emotional.

What are their aspirations?
This is based on what helps them in their daily life – i.e., what makes things easier, or more enjoyable and efficient? These can be written up as objectives and vary in level of priority:

× REQUIRED - These are the gains which a solution cannot function without.

× EXPECTED – These are the gains we expect from a solution, even if it could work without them.

× DESIRED - These are the gains that we would love to have if we could, but are not expected from a solution.

× UNEXPECTED - These are the features that go beyond what is expected.

Now also list the customer's daily struggles and/or their problems. Describe what is annoying and troubling for your customer. These are the blockers that are preventing your customer from getting their job done. These could be undesired costs or situations, negative emotions or unwanted risks.

× WHAT ARE ALL THE DESIGN CONSIDERATIONS AND CONSTRAINTS OF THE PROBLEM?

× WHAT ARE MUST HAVES INVOLVED IN AN APPROPRIATE SOLUTION?

× WHAT ARE THE POTENTIAL CONSTRAINTS OF THE SOLUTION (E.G. MANUFACTURING COSTS, USER BEHAVIOURS)?

Describe the design **INTENT** of the solution. Do not confuse this with an outcome: you don't have to solve this problem, just be able to point to the direction in which to find a solution. List the motivations, rules, criteria of a concept. This can then be used to inform the DESIGN (the next component).

DESIGN BRIEF EXAMPLE

Jammer is a Group Captain in the Royal Australian Air Force (RAAF) and has commissioned a design team to produce a defence specific practical guide to design thinking. With the intention for it to be given to all personnel inside of the RAAF teaching them to solve real defence problems innovatively.

The guide should be based on the principles of Design Thinking to deliver solutions for Defence problems. This guide is meant to introduce methods which highlight the importance of understanding problems people experience, their concerns, needs and behaviours. It should help define what is needed to solve a defence related issue facing the RAAF. It should uncover insights and allow for people to creatively explore new solutions to the problem or opportunity at hand.

PROJECT BRIEF:	MILITARY DESIGN GAME – TO TEACH DEFENCE ABOUT HOW TO USE DESIGN TO SOLVE THEIR PROBLEMS INNOVATIVELY

PREPARED BY:	JAMMER

FRAME DESIGN INTENT

✗ DESCRIBE WHAT PROBLEM CUSTOMERS ARE HAVING AND WHAT THEY WANT TO ACHIEVE?

✗ WHAT ARE THEIR REQUIREMENTS, EXPECTATIONS, & DESIRES WITH SOLVING THIS PROBLEM?

DEFENCE BY DESIGN GAME

X GAME HAS TO BE INTERACTIVE, INFORMATIVE, INTUITIVE TO USE
X SHOULD BE FUN TO PLAY AND ENGAGING
X NO EXTRA MATERIALS REQUIRED – PLAYERS CONTEXT UNKNOWN
X SPARK INTEREST IN DESIGN
X KEEP COMPLEXITY TO A MINIMUM
X DESIRE TO CREATE NEW IDEAS AND SOLVE REAL PROBLEMS
X AN EASY STEP PROCESS FOR DESIGN TO BE UNDERSTOOD TO THE DISCIPLINARY CONTEXT
X AUDIENCE IS FOR ALL EDUCATIONAL LEVELS

DESIGN CONSIDERATIONS & CONSTRAINTS

✗ WHAT ARE THE RULES, CRITERIA FOR A SUCCESSFUL CONCEPT?

✗ WHAT ARE MUST HAVES INVOLVED IN AN APPROPRIATE SOLUTION?

✗ WHAT ARE THE POTENTIAL CONSTRAINTS OF THE SOLUTION (E.G. MANUFACTURING COSTS, USER BEHAVIOURS)?

PRODUCE, PACKAGE AND POST GAMES ALL OVER THE NATION TO DEFENCE PERSONNEL

X MASS MANUFACTURE (KEEP THE COST UNDER $10 PER GAME
X LIGHTWEIGHT AND EASY TO POST – THIS WILL HAVE SIZE CONSTRAINTS AND CONSIDERATIONS
X INSTRUCTIONS WRITTEN IN LAY ENGLISH TO ACCOMPANY GAME

DRIVING
QUESTIONS

INTENT

What is your value proposition?
A value proposition is a belief from the customer about how your design will deliver value (benefit) to them, and how they will experience and acquire it.

Are there any alternative value propositions you could create that better address the opportunities or challenges identified by your customers?
✗ How could you transition into these new value propositions?

What is the intended outcome of your design?
✗ What do you want your design to achieve?
✗ What kind of impact should your design have on stakeholders?
✗ What are the design constraints involved with the solution?

What sort of difference do you want to make in your customers' lives?
✗ Will your product make any? If not, what can you change?

What will (or might) the solution look and feel like?
✗ How will it solve your customers' problems?

Map your customer insights to your company strategy. How do they compare?
✗ Does this work with the current structures? If not, what would you have to change?
✗ Do your current design requirements reflect the current company strategy?
✗ What new business models are possible from your new solution?

How is success going to be measured?
✗ What metrics could you use to determine if your design does what you intended?

DESIGN

DESIGN

The **DESIGN** component is about conceiving and developing an idea that meets your **INTENT**. Now that you have framed what you are endeavouring to accomplish, and the types of outcomes you are hoping to create, you can begin to think about how this could be done.

The goal of this book isn't to offer instructions for designing, but rather to help build an understanding of the broader environment in which design happens. With such an understanding the design can become better informed, and designers can be conscious of the **INTENT** to be achieved. In practice, many organisations believe that an app (or some other popular design of the time) is the answer to all their struggles. Unfortunately, this is not the case, and each challenge and opportunity presents a unique case to be considered.

There will always be the need for new solutions to address the ever-evolving problems that we face. Over time the complexity of our problems has grown; with effective solutions requiring new processes and the involvement of increasingly diverse stakeholders. Globalisation, discovery and development of new technology, and the ongoing difficulties of project and people management has seen the role of the designer evolve to address such problems. However, we must stop and ask how many of the solutions created actually address our stakeholders' problems; are we just designing solutions for the sake of solution creation? A design output, whether required or not, is the result of a long and often difficult journey. Regardless, if you are designing a door handle or national health system, certain steps would have been taken to ensure a successful output.

There are innumerable design processes and frameworks (as discussed earlier in the book), each with its own strengths and weaknesses. However, these processes and frameworks are generally comprised of similar structures.

GENERAL OVERVIEW OF MOST DESIGN PROCESS:

1. A DEFINITION OF THE PROBLEM AT HAND (WHETHER A CHALLENGE OR OPPORTUNITY)

2. AN UNDERSTANDING OF THE STAKEHOLDERS

3. THE CONCEPTUALISATION OF SOLUTIONS

4. PROTOTYPING AND TESTING WHETHER THE SOLUTIONS WORK.

As we've stressed before, design cannot be a prescribed process. This would be a major flaw. Each design project is unique, and you will need to develop expertise and skills to guide it (you wouldn't expect an amateur cook to create a Michelin-star dish just by following a recipe). Thankfully, that is why we've written this book. We're not seers though, so we don't have all the answers. We do, however, have some basic tenets for you to consider while you design. These should put you on the right track and help you focus on developing the right skills. Within business, the entire chain of design, from problem discovery to implementation, needs to be managed. But where to start – well, first, there are many different types of problems that may not even benefit from a design approach. Remember, it is not a silver bullet.

If the problem statement is ill-defined or does not give all the information needed to arrive at a viable solution, more investigation into the problem may be sought. This requires us to find the necessary information to either re-frame or scope out the parameters of the problem before a solution can be designed. The number of potential solutions can be daunting, and you will need to test a number of these to find the right one. Don't make assumptions based on your opinions, actually test what you have come up with. Make sure to ask:

- ✕ DOES THE PROBLEM STATEMENT HAVE ONLY ONE POSSIBLE FIT FOR PURPOSE SOLUTION?
- ✕ HOW WELL DOES THE SOLUTION ADDRESS THE INTENT?

At the start of a project, very little may be known about the solution. As work progresses on the project, knowledge about the problem, and context increases. Therefore, after completing a project, most designers want a chance to start all over again and do things "properly" now that they fully understand it. Unfortunately, this is rarely possible.

Our focus for the component of **DESIGN** has not been on providing a 3-5 step process (as we have already established why this would be problematic, but we encourage you to do some further reading on these if you are new to design). We wish to take a more practical approach to design, therefore we believe the core aspect for it is **SKILLS** (rather than a process).

SKILLS

CORE **SKILLS**

Design is not a set of tools or methods you can simply complete, with the expectation that (magically) an innovative solution will appear. Along with the surge of design popularity so too comes the popularity of design buzzwords. Some you might have heard of are idea generation (brain dumping), design-led agile thinking innovation (multiple popular methods combined), breakthrough innovations (creating something no one has ever thought of before), disruptive innovation (a term for an excuse to blow things up and be very disorganised). Designers don't use these terms. The thing to remember is that design was done before design thinking was a thing (check out the 200 years of design and innovation timeline). Designers have evidence of design outcomes, practice, sketches – these are all things that can be improved upon. It's messy and requires proof. There is no set time limits, no instructions, no required resources nor post-it notes required to design. Design is a craft, requiring technique, intuition and expertise. Therefore, we believe the core of design to be **SKILLS**, with the 3 of the most basic skills being:

X · VISUALISATION
X · CREATIVITY
X · CONSTRUCTION AND DESTRUCTION

VISUALISATION

Sketching is not a step but a vital part of the entire process Liedtka and Ogilvie (2011) refers to visualisation as the 'mother of all design tools' (core element in their ten design thinking methods) explaining that visualisation is about imagining; as images provide understanding more quickly and effectively than words alone. Visualisation, as a process, replaces text and numbers with images, maps and stories, allowing ideas to be understood by a wider audience. Activities such as sketching are what most people understand as 'designing', but these are merely iterative steps in the grand scheme of design. Both formal and informal sketching are necessary through all the stages of design. Industrial designers, for instance, are taught product sketching and are skilled in making and interpreting design ideas. Sketches also facilitate communication with other members or stakeholders in a project and can help to develop and think through an idea (e.g., by creating 'napkin

SKETCHING IS NOT A STEP BUT A VITAL PART IN THE ENTIRE PROCESS.

sketches' of rough ideas, which can be particularly useful for sharing ideas early on). The visual outputs of sketching or digital rendering can be a huge advantage in future-oriented projects, as they are able present visions of the future that break existing norms and expectations. Images are able to communicate abstract concepts into usable, tangible and concrete solutions. Visualisation can also communicate complex systems on a single page, allowing multiple perspectives to be shared and developed together, quickly making abstract ideas more tangible (Evans, 2011).

CREATIVITY

Creativity has regularly been referenced as a skill required for the workforce of the next generation, due largely to the fact that creativity is a skill that is yet to be replaced by robots (World Economic Forum, 2019). 'Thinking outside the box' is a term commonly used when explaining what creativity is, requiring the ability to see and approach things in different ways. Creativity is required throughout all parts of a design process, but most importantly in concept development. This is an energetic and exciting part of the process – but can also quickly become frustrating and gruelling when you hit a 'creative block'. Creativity should result in a range of possible solutions by looking at the problem from a variety of perspectives. All of which should be continually traced back to the design **INTENT**. Creativity is discussed more in **THINKING STYLES** later in the book.

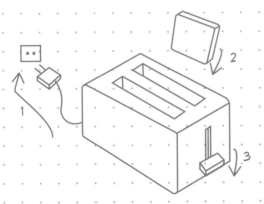

(CON/DE) STRUCTION

Generally, after the concept development stage, feedback from stakeholders is sought and the iterative process begins again. We refer to this skill as construction and destruction as it requires you to build and break your ideas (a difficult thing for many people to do). Also referred to as prototyping, this process should be iterative, with each iteration becoming more focused as more is learned. The intended solution isn't the only thing you can prototype.

Next time you design, consider prototyping other aspects of a project such as (Miller, 2005):

× A CONCEPTUAL MODEL
   Do users understand it? Does it make sense?
× FUNCTIONALITY
   Does it do what is needed?
× TERMINOLOGY
   Do users understand the terms you use?
× SYSTEM
   Does the solution fit within a system?
× IMPLEMENTATION
   How will it be achieved?

Just like a design process, multiple methods exist for prototyping. Visual simulations, for example, can be used for walking users through the experience of the concept. Storyboards and photo narratives can provide a narrative of the intended interactions and use of a solution or explain the problem and how the solution addresses it. Visual mock-ups created in computer-aided software can be used to develop a high-fidelity model of the solution.

There are countless **SKILLS** that we could cover alongside the three selected for this chapter. Two of these are of interest, as we believe that they are fundamentals and often overlooked: design philosophy and practice, and design critique and criteria. These are both outlined in the next sections. We have also included a number of other tools in the back of the book to either get your creative juices flowing **(DESIGNING INNOVATIVE PRODUCTS, CIRCLE CREATION, INNOVATION MASHING AND MR. SQUIGGLE)**, help you develop basic visual communication skills **(POST-IT NOTE PICTIONARY AND LETTERS AND NUMBERS)** and get you to construct and destruct successfully **(PROTOTYPE PLAN)**.

A GREAT RESOURCE BOOK ON DESIGN METHODS, TOOLS AND APPROACHES TO HAVE IS THE DELFT DESIGN GUIDE.

DESIGN ISN'T MAGIC.
BUT IT IS MAGICAL!

DESIGN PHILOSOPHY AND PRACTICE

We believe that being a good designer starts with establishing a practice which is guided by design philosophy. A strong philosophy can be seen guiding many influential and successful designers throughout time (check out the 200 years of design and innovation timeline for some inspiration). You may have been asked to design in the manner of a particular designer, taking on their identifiable features and practices. This is generally the start to developing your own design practice, you begin with analysing and embracing the style of great designers in order to learn and develop your own practice.

Your design philosophy may require you to have technical skills and a well-developed aesthetic appreciation. Colour, texture, form, line, space can be considered 'tools of the trade' for designers. Particular projects might see you become an expert in ergonomics or require you to understand basic behavioural science. This should all be part of you forming your own design philosophy. Understanding and embracing different knowledge and skills will make you a better designer over time. Norman (1988) highlights there is a link between better designers and better design, believing that the intentions of the designer are expressed through the design. And, according to Norman (1988), the way to have better designs is to have more enlightened designers.

In practice we tend to place more emphasis on the output of design rather than the act of designing (which makes sense, customers usually see the product they are buying, not how it was designed). However, this devalues what it means to design and is a barrier to becoming a better designer; how can you improve the way you design if you never take the time to consider your design practice?

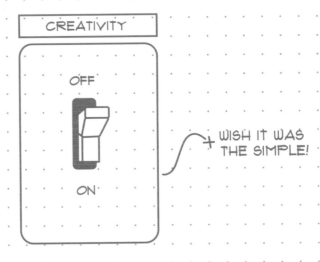

To start the process of understanding and creating your philosophy and overall design practice we turn to one of the most known design philosophies (or principles) by Dieter Rams. His 10 Good Design Principles has inspired a generation of designers. Design principles can be used to guide your design practice and decisions and distinguish you from the crowd. These should develop and change as you become more experienced. You could have one principle or 100, it's up to you to decide. If you are new to the game start with Ram's 10 good design principles (below) (De Jong, 2017). As he created these in the 1960s and 1970s, you first need to question (agree or disagree) if they are still 'good' principles for designing in the 21st century (go on write on the side of the page!). This should give you a better understanding of what a design philosophy is and help you understand what should be considered when creating a 'good' design. The second part of the tool, **DEFINING YOUR PHILOSOPHY**, gets you to state your design principles. Give each of them a name and write a description, which clearly explains what the principle entails. Alternatively, you can frame principles as statements which explain what design means to you and how you wish to practice it (e.g., the design principle of 'sustainability' could be used to communicate your passion for the environment and desire to positively impact it).

DIETER RAM'S 'GOOD' DESIGN PRINCIPLES. GOOD DESIGN...

IS INNOVATIVE	THE POSSIBILITIES FOR INNOVATION ARE NOT, BY ANY MEANS, EXHAUSTIVE. TECHNOLOGICAL DEVELOPMENT IS ALWAYS OFFERING NEW OPPORTUNITIES FOR INNOVATIVE DESIGN. BUT INNOVATIVE DESIGN ALWAYS DEVELOPS IN TANDEM WITH INNOVATIVE TECHNOLOGY, AND CAN NEVER BE AN END IN ITSELF.
MAKES A PRODUCT USEFUL	A PRODUCT IS BOUGHT TO BE USED. IT HAS TO SATISFY CERTAIN CRITERIA, NOT ONLY FUNCTIONAL, BUT ALSO PSYCHOLOGICAL AND AESTHETIC. GOOD DESIGN EMPHASISES THE USEFULNESS OF A PRODUCT WHILST DISREGARDING ANYTHING THAT COULD POSSIBLY DETRACT FROM IT.
IS AESTHETIC	THE AESTHETIC QUALITY OF A PRODUCT IS INTEGRAL TO ITS USEFULNESS BECAUSE PRODUCTS WE USE EVERY DAY AFFECT OUR PERSON AND OUR WELL-BEING. BUT ONLY WELL-EXECUTED OBJECTS CAN BE BEAUTIFUL
MAKES A PRODUCT UNDERSTANDABLE	IT CLARIFIES THE PRODUCTS STRUCTURE. BETTER STILL, IT CAN MAKE THE PRODUCT TALK. AT BEST, IT IS SELF-EXPLANATORY.
IS HONEST	IT DOES NOT MAKE A PRODUCT MORE INNOVATIVE, POWERFUL OR VALUABLE THAN IT REALLY IS. IT DOES NOT ATTEMPT TO MANIPULATE THE CONSUMER WITH PROMISES THAT CANNOT BE KEPT.
IS LONG-LASTING	IT AVOIDS BEING FASHIONABLE AND THEREFORE NEVER APPEARS ANTIQUATED. UNLIKE FASHIONABLE DESIGN, IT LASTS MANY YEARS – EVEN IN TODAYS THROWAWAY SOCIETY.
IS THOROUGH DOWN TO THE LAST DETAIL	NOTHING MUST BE ARBITRARY OR LEFT TO CHANCE. CARE AND ACCURACY IN THE DESIGN PROCESS SHOW RESPECT OF THE CONSUMER.
IS ENVIRONMENTALLY FRIENDLY	DESIGN MAKES AN IMPORTANT CONTRIBUTION TO THE PRESERVATION OF THE ENVIRONMENT. IT CONSERVES RESOURCES AND MINIMISES PHYSICAL AND VISUAL POLLUTION THROUGHOUT THE LIFECYCLE OF THE PRODUCT.
INVOLVES AS LITTLE DESIGN AS POSSIBLE	LESS, BUT BETTER – BECAUSE IT CONCENTRATES ON THE ESSENTIAL ASPECTS, AND THE PRODUCTS ARE NOT BURDENED WITH NON-ESSENTIALS. BACK TO PURITY, BACK TO SIMPLICITY.
IS UNOBTRUSIVE	PRODUCTS FULFILLING A PURPOSE ARE LIKE TOOLS. THEY ARE NEITHER DECORATIVE OBJECTS NOR WORKS OF ART. THEIR DESIGN SHOULD THEREFORE BE BOTH NEUTRAL AND RESTRAINED, TO LEAVE ROOM FOR THE USER'S SELF-EXPRESSION.

DESIGN PRACTICE

You can use the tool **VISUALISE YOUR PRACTICE** to understand how you view design. First start by adding your definition of what design is. This could be a general statement or something relevant to a particular project or design brief you are working on. For the next step, think about your design practice, how do you start it? Where does it end? Is it simple or does it have lots of parts which could all lead in different directions? You can begin by writing it out, but make sure to use the space to visualise it – this is an important part of the tool, as it requires you question how your practice can be represented by images (a great chance to work on your visualisation skills!). We suggest you do this at start of every project and then again at the end, to learn how your practice may have or may need to change (or not).

EXAMPLES OF VISUAL DESIGN PRACTICES

UK DESIGN COUNCIL 'DOUBLE DIAMOND' MODEL:

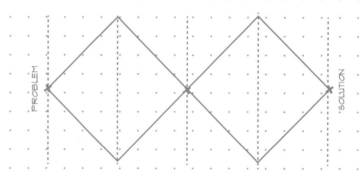

DESIGN SQUIGGLE BY DAMIEN NEWMAN:

THE 'IDEO' MODEL:

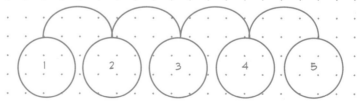

THE SIX (REAL) STAGES OF DESIGN PRACTICE:

1. EXCITEMENT
2. PROCRASTINATION
3. PANIC
4. CRYING
5. EUREKA
6. DEADLINE ✗

ALSO KNOWN AS "RESEARCHING" VIA NETFLIX

USUALLY IN THE MIDDLE OF THE NIGHT!

PUSHED BACK 3 TIMES ALREADY

ARE THEY BEING A 'BAD' DESIGNER CHECKLIST:

☐ THEY ARE ACTING LIKE A LONE RANGER (PRACTING WHAT IS PREACHED IN A DESIGN PROCESS- CHOOSING THEIR IDEAS OVER OTHERS)

☐ THEY DON'T DEFER JUDGEMENT

☐ THEY AREN'T TAKING ANY RISKS, ALWAYS PLAYING IT SAFE

☐ THEY HAVEN'T CREATED A 'SAFE' CREATIVE SPACE

☐ THEY ARE TAKING THEMSELVES TOO SERIOUSLY

☐ THEY ARE BEING A DICK

☐ THEY CALL THEMSELVES AN 'INNOVATOR OR ENTREPRENEUR' WHILE BEING EXTREMELY RISK AVERSE

☐ DON'T RECOGNISE THAT FAILURE = KNOWLEDGE

IF THIS SOUNDS LIKE YOUR BOSS - THE ORGANISATION MAY NOT BE READY FOR THE IMPLEMENTATION OF A DESIGN INNOVATION APPROACH!

DESIGN CRITQUE & CRITERIA

Part of the practice of design is a continuous, rapid and repeated sequence of analysis, synthesis and evaluation (McNeill et all. 1998). This is something a designer learns (very quickly) at any good design school, usually in the form of a studio design critique. This is where one person shares their ideas or design concepts with others (usually other designers) to get valuable feedback. Often this feedback is brutally honest and can feel overly harsh the first few times you go through it. Designers quickly learn how to get a thicker skin. You learn how to disassociate from your design and think (and see) it objectively. This builds resilience and makes for a better, more confident designer. You learn how to handle criticism and not get defensive when receiving feedback. This is a critical step for any designer. Without this the design cannot be improved or move forward in its conceptualisation and development. A design critique can help you determine:

✕ · HOW TO CHOOSE BETWEEN DIFFERENT DESIGNS

✕ · HOW TO DECIDE IF ONE IDEA IS BETTER THAN ANOTHER

✕ · HOW TO MEASURE IF ANY IDEA IS BETTER THAN ANOTHER

The general use of 'critique' means a systematic and objective examination of an idea, phenomenon, or artifact, however, within design this also includes an evaluation of an idea as well as the act itself (Hokanson, 2012). These are not easy endeavours, and in reality, will not lead to a clear outcome. They will likely just lead you to just ask more questions. It is the designer's role to know which design will provide the most value to the user or customer. A way to support this process is to create a set of design criteria.

KEY FEATURES WHICH MAKE A DESIGN CRITIQUE:

☐ REQUIRES CRITICAL THINKING

☐ IDENTIFIES HOW A DESIGN MEETS OR DOESN'T MEET A NEED

☐ DELIVERS ACTIONABLE STEPS TO TAKE TO IMPROVE THE DESIGN

☐ CREATES AN ENVIRONMENT FOR ACTIVE DISCUSSION (WHERE EVERY OPINION IS VALID)

☐ SHOULD LEAVE YOU EMPOWERED + WANTING TO IMPROVE YOUR DESIGN

☐ REQUIRES EVERYONE TO ACCEPT THE GOAL IS TO IMPROVE THE DESIGN AND NOT TO PUT SOMEONE DOWN

☐ MUST INCLUDE THE REASONING OR LOGIC BEHIND A STATEMENT OR QUESTION (SIMPLY SAYING 'I HATE IT' DOES NOT COUNT AS A CRITIQUE BUT IS SIMPLY SHARING AN OPINION).

DESIGN CRITIQUE

LEARNING FROM FEEDBACK

DESIGN CRITERIA are explicit goals that the design much achieve to be considered successful. Pitt (2008, 318), when discussing architectural design states, explains that 'before we design the space, we ought to have some criteria to guide our design'. This demonstrates that having criteria will increase the probability that the design will be successful in achieving its goal. Pitt (2008) continues to explain that criteria serves two purposes:

1. GUIDE THE DESIGN
2. TO BE THE FACTORS BY WHICH THE SUCCESS OF DESIGN IS JUDGED.

Criteria can be divided into primary and secondary criterions. Primary criteria can be described as "must haves", while secondary could be described as "nice to haves" – they are highly desirable but not essential for success. Separating criteria into these two groups can assist you to create a hierarchy and help guide design decisions. Use the tool **DESIGN CRITERIA** to start exploring what your design needs. First, give each criteria a catchy name, then provide a short description and classification (is it primary or secondary?).

Some quick tips for writing your criteria include:

✗ KEEP THEM SHORT BUT AS SPECIFIC AS POSSIBLE
✗ AVOID VAGUE OR FLUFFY LANGUAGE
✗ LIST PRIMARY CRITERIA FIRST.

Several tools are available for evaluating designs. We present the **SOLUTION EVALUATION** tool, which is based off the seminal work of Harris (1964). Specifically, Harris's work on visually representing the strengths and weaknesses of design concepts so they can be evaluated and compared. Over time, this has evolved into a more nuanced version with scoring. Solution evaluation, like many other scorecards, lists pre-defined requirements (criteria) which allow a clear benchmark to be drawn between solutions (design concepts). This method works well with teams as they can work through the scorecard process collectively, allowing for robust conversations that provide clear directions for design.

The purpose of this tool is to visually, quickly and easily benchmark multiple design solutions and evaluate how well they meet your intent and the criteria set. Using the tool **SOLUTION EVALUATION**, list your criteria in the first column and sketch each of your solutions in the boxes in the first row. Then for each solution, go through the criteria and (in the space next to each criterion) provide a short explanation of how it (or how it doesn't) meet the defined criterion. Once each solution has been critiqued add notes on how each solution could be adjusted to fulfil any criteria that were not met. This tool is a visual way to complete a general evaluation of a design, and to further guide design decisions. The use of this tool will allow you evaluate different projects across multiple criteria. The evaluation of a design should not be based on personal intuition alone, but on predetermined criteria that investigate the viability, feasibility and desirability of a concept or solution.

DRIVING QUESTIONS

DESIGN

Conceptualise and visualise three possible design solutions that meet your customers' needs.

✗ *Explain how each solution addresses your customers' needs.*

✗ *Mock-up some user-scenarios for your design.*

How will you conceptualise, prototype and test your solution(s)?

✗ *What is the focus of the prototype? E.g., conceptual model, functionality, terminology, or implementation.*

How can your proposed solution take advantage of your current business strengths?

✗ *What would have to change inside your organisation to best support this solution?*

Have you created a set of criteria (objectives) that your design needs to meet?

✗ *What features in your design are must-haves, nice-to-haves and/or could be removed?*

✗ *What would it take for your solution to work?*

✗ *How is the solution addressing the customers' needs?*

✗ *Which concept best meets all the criteria and why?*

How will you ensure that your solution will be critiqued?

✗ *Have you set-up critiques to be performed throughout the design process?*

✗ *Who will be involved in the critiques? Stakeholders? Peers?*

Are there any other products on the market that are similar to your new design?

EMENT

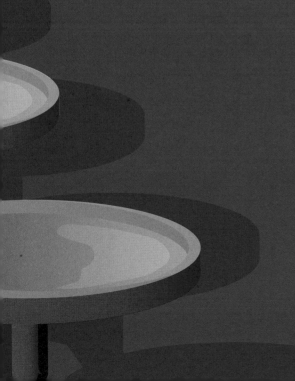

IMPLEMENT

The outcome of **DESIGN** is usually an idea or concept (with varying degrees of development). **IMPLEMENT**ing design refers to converting the idea (your concept) into something real (like something you could buy in a store). It is about bringing design into the 'real world', and is perhaps the most difficult component of all the stages in design innovation (Nusem, Straker & Wrigley, 2020). Coming up with an idea (good or bad) is relatively simple. Turning that idea into reality is a whole other matter. Many people have good ideas, but very few of these good ideas are implemented into practice. Translating design into practice involves factors such as:

X MARKET ENTRY STRATEGY
X PLAN FOR GROWTH AND SCALING
X DEVELOPING AN ECOSYSTEM IN WHICH THE SOLUTION CAN THRIVE.

Implementation is the key term here, as many design thinking methods, toolkits and sprints will focus mainly on the generation of ideas – whereas design innovation also focuses on design doing. I.e., how to progress beyond just having an idea. Our argument for the inclusion of the **IMPLEMENT** component, is that designs that do not consider an implementation plan are rarely implemented. As a designer, you need to be cognisant of this. This stage provides designers the opportunity to expand their foundational design skills and engage in the logistics of commercialising their designs.

Implementation involves identifying how the project can be funded and demonstrating that a project can become an economically sustainable solution (Hultink, Griffin, Hart & Robben, 1997). Often such considerations are undertaken separate to design practice. However, considering the business implications of a solution at the time of design development will help the final solution meet the needs of both the user and organisation.

The implementation phase must address four key issues:
1. WHAT TO LAUNCH (IS A NEW PRODUCT, SERVICE OR COMPLETE SYSTEM?)
2. WHEN TO LAUNCH (WHAT IS THE MOST APPROPRIATE TIME DO IT?)
3. HOW TO LAUNCH (WHAT IS REQUIRED TO MAKE IT HAPPEN?)
4. WHY IT SHOULD BE LAUNCHED (WHAT ARE THE BENEFITS).

These decisions involve significant commitments of time, money and resources. They also go a long way toward determining the success or failure of any proposed solution. These questions are usually addressed and presented in what is known as a business case. However, such business cases alone do not constitute implementation – it is merely the blueprint for getting approval.

Implementation is closely aligned to the theory of new product development (NPD) which is concerned with the process of bringing a product or service to market. It has been previously established that the fields of marketing, strategy and design are key contributors to the new product development process (Kotler, 2003; Kahn, 2013; Bruce and Bessant, 2002). Designers play various roles within this process from the maker to the marketer. However, the ability a designer to not only see the bigger picture in terms of the solution; but also confidently present it so it will become a reality. We therefore have placed **COMMUNICATION** as the core aspect of **IMPLEMENT.**

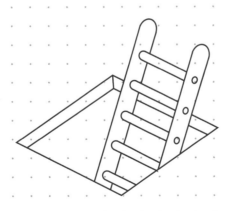

COMMUNICATION

CORE
COMMUNICATION

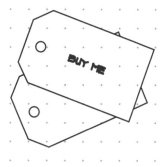

The core aspect of **IMPLEMENT** is communication. Implementation will require buy-in (from the organisation or investors), which means that your ability to communicate the value of a solution is essential. Good communication can be the bridge between an idea and implementation. While we frame this as the core aspect for implementation, communicating is something that you should be doing across every component in the design innovation framework.

Design can be judged based on desirability (do customers want it), feasibility (is it technologically sound) and viability (is there a clear financial benefit) (Brown, 2008). Naturally, companies tend to focus on viability. Communicating the viability of the idea or solution to multiple stakeholders (both internally and externally) can be difficult, as it is not only about selling them the merits of the idea but the viability of it. This is the solution's ability to generate profit and/or value to the organisation or investors. To have a shot at implementation, you should be able to communicate how:

- ✗ you are going to make the design a reality
- ✗ the organisation is going to make money out of the design
- ✗ the investment can be justified
- ✗ you are going to sell this up the organisation's value chain.

Communication and getting buy-in along the way can be difficult, challenging and at times feels like it's half the battle. This is why it is important to remain focused on the broader context and to reinforce the core value for stakeholders' in your communications. The best solution in the world won't succeed if you are unable to describe the value it will create. To guide you in this process we outline constructing a **BUSINESS CASE** and **PITCHING**, two tools we think are vital in the **IMPLEMENT** component. We have also included the **PRODUCT CLASSIFICATION MATRIX**, **3-HORIZON GROWTH STRATEGY** and **JOHNSON & JONES MATRIX** as supplementary tools to support building your **IMPLEMENT** strategy.

A **PITCH** is key soft skill for designers. It can help you 'sell' an idea or concept to the audience, to promote yourself (for example in an interview), to get buy-in for a design, or to secure funding from investors (Daly & Davy, 2015). At its core, it is about persuading and convincing your audience. The keys to a successful pitch are passion, knowing your audience, being clear about objectives, and to think about benefits rather than features (Varga, 2009). No two pitches should be the same, but the following steps should help you to prepare.

1. PREPARE YOURSELF, NOT JUST YOUR IDEA.

Investors don't just invest in a solid business plan, they also invest in the person responsible for that plan. You will need to demonstrate that you are fast, thoughtful, resourceful and efficient, and that you can sustain the project through its conception and growth. The first impression counts, so make sure that you come across as confident and capable. Dress sharp and be prepared (some more tips on how to prepare are listed in step 5):

PEOPLE INVEST IN PEOPLE
(THINK ABOUT HOW YOU CAN PRO-TRAY THE
FOLLOWING THROUGH YOUR PITCH)

X INTEGRITY   X LEADERSHIP
X PASSION   X COMMITMENT
X EXPERIENCE   X VISION
X KNOWLEDGE   X REALISM
X SKILL   X LEARNING AND ADAPTING

2. CAPTURE THE ESSENTIALS

Investors care just as much about the presentation as they do the business plan, so you need to make sure that your presentation covers all of the essentials. There are two key considerations here. The first is the audience. You'll need to identify who they are, what kind of presentation style they are used to, what kind of beliefs and principles they have and what they will find compelling. Don't assume you know these things, as not everyone will have the same preferences as you. The second is consideration of what to communicate. Before putting your presentation together you should outline what the most important aspects are, and how important each of these aspects is.

UNDERSTAND YOUR AUDIENCE
X WHO ARE THEY?
X WHAT ARE THEIR ROLES?
X WHAT IS THEIR BACKGROUND & EXPERTISE?

Most design pitches have similar content and can be expected to cover:

- ✗ WHAT IS THE PROBLEM OR OPPORTUNITY? BE SPECIFIC.
- ✗ HOW BIG IS THE PROBLEM OR OPPORTUNITY? THIS IS ABOUT ESTABLISHING WHY ITS RELEVANT.
- ✗ WHY IS THIS A PROBLEM OR OPPORTUNITY? SHARE YOUR INSIGHTS ABOUT THIS CONTEXT.
- ✗ WHAT IS THE SOLUTION? ESTABLISH HOW THE PROBLEM OR OPPORTUNITY COULD BE ADDRESSED.
- ✗ HOW DOES IT WORK? PROVIDE EVIDENCE FOR YOUR SOLUTION.
- ✗ WHAT VALUE DOES IT BRING TO THE CUSTOMER/USER/STAKEHOLDERS? SHOW WHY YOUR SOLUTION IS GOOD.

3. TELL IT IN A STORY

Pitches can get pretty repetitive. As designers, we have access to information and skills that other professions often overlook; we are great storytellers. Framing your pitch through a story about a person (or persona) can help it stand out and facilitate building empathy with the audience. To do so, you must first select the perspective you wish to share, this could be a customer, the company, or something else entirely. Then explain, through their perspective:

- ✗ THE NEED/PROBLEM/OPPORTUNITY AND CONTEXT (THE ADDRESSABLE MARKET NEED)
- ✗ THE USER, ALONG WITH WHAT THEY GAIN YOU ARE SEEKING TO CREATE OR WHAT PAIN YOU ARE SEEKING TO RELIEVE FOR THEM
- ✗ THE SOLUTION (PRODUCT, SYSTEM, SERVICE, ETC.) THAT WILL CREATE THE GAIN OR RELIEVE THE PAIN, HOW IT WORKS AND ON WHAT SCALE
- ✗ THE VALUE (TO THE USER / COMPANY / SOCIETY) THAT THE SOLUTION WILL CREATE

Remember that most people that you will pitch to will have likely seen an exorbitant number of pitches. They will be quite desensitised, so you will need provide a specific user scenario that is compelling — a novel way of introducing your story. A good pitch is more than words, so think about how you could visually bring the solution to life (for example by using pictures or videos). Its not always required, but can be good practice to note how you are positioned against competitors.

COMMUNICATING A PROBLEM OR OPPORTUNITY OUT OF CONTEXT IS VERY DIFFERENT TO SHARING IT THROUGH THE PERSPECTIVE OF SPECIFIC PERSON (E.G. BY STARTING YOUR PRESENTATION BY SAYING "MEET" JERRY. JERRY IS...), WHICH CAN HELP PEOPLE BUILD EMPATHY.

4. STRUCTURE THE PITCH

Pitches vary greatly in length. We recommend that you think about creating a 5-second, 30-second and 5-minute version of your pitch. The elevator pitch (5 seconds) is the most concise, single-sentence formulation of whatever your idea is. While very short, it is probably the most difficult kind of pitch as every word counts. Refine, refine, refine your thinking until you can say something intelligent and interesting in a short sentence (Berkun, 2010). This can be done for any idea: never allow yourself to believe that what you are pitching is so complicated and amazing that it's impossible to explain in one sentence. The 30-second and 5-minute versions should grow naturally out of the 5 second version. In 30 seconds there's enough time to talk about how you'll achieve what you described in 5 seconds, or to provide specifics on how the 2-3 most significant things would be achieved. The 5-minute pitch allows you to provide more detail, just enough that the listener can get a clearer picture of your idea, and gain a deeper and more nuanced understanding of what you're proposing.

TO START YOUR THINKING

WRITE YOUR SOLUTION IN ONE SENTENCE

'MY IDEA? IT'S A WAY TO MAKE CAR ENGINES TWICE AS EFFICIENT, AND 5 TIMES AS POWERFUL.'

ILLUSTRATE THIS SENTENCE ONLY USING IMAGES

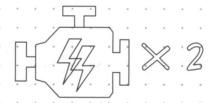

WRITE A TITLE AND A SUPPORTING PHRASE FOR THE SOLUTION

CREATE A DISTINCTIVE AND COMPELLING TITLE FOR THE PROPOSED INNOVATION. JUST AS IN A SLOGAN, IN A FEW WORDS, WRITE A SHORT SUPPORTING PHRASE TO CONCISELY EXPRESS THE ESSENCE OF THE SOLUTION.

WRITE SHORT DESCRIPTIONS OF PAINS AND GAINS

WRITE A SHORT DESCRIPTION ABOUT THE CHALLENGES (PROBLEMS) BEING ADDRESSED BY YOUR PROJECT. IN PARALLEL, WRITE ABOUT HOW THE INNOVATION SOLUTIONS RESPOND TO THESE CHALLENGES & WHAT BENEFITS (VALUE) THEY BRING.

5. DO YOUR HOMEWORK

You don't have to reinvent the wheel for every pitch. It's not bad practice to see how others have pitched ideas in the past, and this can help you identify some interesting, memorable and unique ways of pitching to grab the audience's attention. We can't stress this enough, but as the saying goes: 'practice makes perfect'. You need to know your pitch like the back of your hand. This will come naturally as you objectively review your presentation, but it also won't hurt to do some dry runs.

When reviewing your work, consider the following:
X DOES THE PRESENTATION MAKE SENSE IN THIS ORDER?
X HAVE YOU USED LAY TERMS TO DESCRIBE THE SOLUTION?
X IS YOUR VALUE PROPOSITION CLEARLY COMMUNICATED?
X ARE YOU CONFIDENT IN YOUR ABILITY TO PRESENT?
X CAN YOU CONVINCE THE AUDIENCE THAT THIS IS A VIABLE SOLUTION?

A pitch doesn't end when you finish your presentation. Your audience will likely have some questions. Take time before your presentation to think about what these questions might be so that you can deftly answer them when they come up. Getting familiar with your audience should help you hypothesise what questions might come up. Now that we have outlined what to do, it is time to consider what not to do.

IF YOU'RE LOOKING FOR INSPIRATION CHECK
OUT SOME SUCCESSFUL CAMPAIGNS AND
PITCHES FROM THESE KICKSTARTER, POZIBLE
AND/OR SHARK TANK.

PITCH CHECKLIST:

☐ KNOW YOUR AUDIENCE

☐ REMOVE ANY ACRONYMS

☐ EXCLUDED ANY UNTRUTHS OR UNSUBSTANTIATED STATEMENTS

☐ ENSURED THERE ARE NO INCONSISTENCIES IN THE FINAL DESIGN SOLUTION

☐ MADE SURE NOT TO CRITICISE THE TECHNOLOGY, RESEARCHERS, COMPANY OR INVESTORS YOU ARE PRESENTING TO

☐ HAVE AN INTERESTING WAY TO START THE PITCH SO YOU STAND OUT FROM THE CROWD

☐ YOU HAVE MEMORISED YOUR PITCH (NO READING OFF A SCRIPT- THIS WILL GUARANTEE THAT PEOPLE WILL ASSUME YOU ARE UNFAMILIAR WITH YOUR CONTENT).

Much like a pitch, a **BUSINESS CASE** is about telling a compelling story about a business need (the problem or opportunity you are seeking to solve) that shows the potential risks and returns. As established by Sheen and Gallo (2013), every good story has characters:

✕ YOUR STAKEHOLDERS are who will approve or reject your business case. It could be your boss, your boss's boss, or someone else from your organisation's senior leadership team

✕ BENEFICIARIES are who will benefit from what you're proposing. They can be inside or outside the organisation, and there will likely be several groups

✕ SUBJECT-MATTER EXPERTS are those that will help you create the case. They will have insight into how the problem will be solved or have expertise which you are lacking (e.g., colleagues from R&D, sales, and marketing, or someone from finance that will help with cost estimates).

A business case that doesn't consider these characters isn't going to get very far, so keep them in mind as you put your business case together. An entire book could be written about how to put a business case together (and many have!), so we are just going to focus on a few select aspects. The key elements for a business case are:

✕ EXECUTIVE SUMMARY
✕ THE DESIGN SOLUTION AND NEED
✕ MARKET SIZE AND SHARE
✕ COMPETITIVE ADVANTAGE
✕ INTELLECTUAL PROPERTY PROTECTION STRATEGY
✕ MARKET ENTRY STRATEGY
✕ FUNDING REQUIREMENTS
✕ POTENTIAL RISKS AND RETURNS.

These are not exhaustive, and this is not the prescribed order. Remember that a business case is a narrative, so you will need to determine how to make it flow organically and logically.

An executive summary should incorporate three components: the need, the solution and the impact (Sheen & Gallo, 2013). Take the following example for instance:

"NEW ENTRANTS IN OUR EUROPEAN MARKET HAVE SIGNIFICANTLY REDUCED OUR MARKET SHARE" [THE NEED]

WE'VE DESIGNED A NEW SERVICE THAT SHOULD HELP US REGAIN THAT MARKET [THE SOLUTION]

IF LAUNCHED, WE EXPECT SALES TO INCREASE BY 150% IN THE FIRST TWO MONTHS, WHICH WILL ALLOW US TO RECOUP THE INVESTMENT WITHIN TWO YEARS [THE IMPACT]

It's a concise story with a hook, that clearly communicates what you are doing and why you are doing it. Of course, this type of executive summary structure is great for an intrapreneur. An entrepreneur will also have to demonstrate the industry and context.

The **DESIGN SOLUTION AND NEED** will provide an overview of the design and the need (problem or opportunity) it corresponds to. This could be a product, service, system or process. It should communicate the features and benefits of your design, and clearly articulate how these address the needs of your beneficiaries. Try not to rely on words, a visual representation of your design solution can really help your business case stand out.

MARKET SIZE AND SHARE is where you will identify what segment of the market you will be targeting, along with how prevalent this segment is. It is a good opportunity to identify the different profiles and archetypes in the market and to justify your selection. This is also a great place to discuss your competitors and their positioning, and to demonstrate if the market is growing.

Your **COMPETITIVE ADVANTAGE** should outline how you will deliver superior value (in relation to competitors) to your beneficiaries. It should have a clear link to the problem or opportunity you are addressing, and answer why an investor or stakeholder would be interested in your design. Ideally, you should also demonstrate why your competitive advantage would be hard to replicate (is sustainable), as this will help the decision makers weigh the potential risks and rewards.

INTELLECTUAL PROPERTY PROTECTION STRATEGY ties in well to the replicability we just discussed. This aspect will help the reader understand how you will protect your idea, and why it would be difficult for competitors to follow in your footsteps. Your intellectual property could be protected through patents, trademark protection, design protection and copyright.

MARKET ENTRY STRATEGY relates to how you plan to distribute or deliver your design to the target market. This can be determined by analysing the newness of your design output in relation to the newness of the market – resulting in four approaches (Ansoff, 1957):

✕ MARKET PENETRATION: aims to increase market share in existing markets with existing products or services (e.g. by reaching your competitor's customers)
✕ PRODUCT DEVELOPMENT: aims to increase demand in existing markets through the new or modified products (e.g. better meeting customer needs through new products)
✕ MARKET DEVELOPMENT: aims to offer existing products or services in new markets (e.g. finding new geographic contexts in which your offerings could be deployed)
✕ DIVERSIFICATION: represents new products in new markets

As we've established; your strategy will depend on your design and market, along with other contextual factors. We recommend that you check out the Ansoff Matrix to help you frame this particular aspect.

FUNDING REQUIREMENTS are your financials. They describe how much funding you will need, when you will need it and how you plan to use it. Amongst others, this could be inclusive of development staffing, resourcing and real estate costs.

Finally, we have the POTENTIAL RISKS AND RETURNS. This is a spectrum which captures the potential return on an investment in relation to the amount of risk undertaken in said investment. It can be communicated in a myriad of ways ranging in complexity and thoroughness. A popular method is calculating the return-on-investment (ROI) and pairing it with a qualitative review of risks. If you identify a risk, do your due diligence and incorporate a risk mitigation strategy.

These elements collectively form the business case, which should help you bypass the first stage-gate for implementation: securing funding from investors or getting buy-in from your organisation.

DRIVING QUESTIONS

IMPLEMENT

What kind of business model does your new solution require?

✗ *What changes are required to be made to your existing model, if any?*

How could the organisation execute the solution?

✗ *What is your path to market strategy?*

How will you pitch the solution to your company and/or investors?

✗ *Have you established a clear, cohesive and compelling narrative?*

✗ *Have you gotten support from those that can help ensure you are able to proceed with your design?*

What are all the possible barriers to implementation or uptake of your solution?

✗ *How could these be overcome?*

✗ *What is the best approach to selling the solution within the company (e.g. bottom-up or top-down) and why?*

What capabilities does your company need to acquire, and what activities does it need to perform, for the solution to be implemented successfully?

Do you require any partnerships to implement the solution?

✗ *If so, how could these be secured and what value would you offer to your partners?*

✗ *How will you implement and/or launch your solution into the marketplace?*

Have you identified and recruited people to champion your design?

How will your solution fit into the current culture of your organisation?

✗ *Will you need to change it or the culture?*

SUPPORT FROM MANAGEMENT OR EXECUTIVES CAN BE A KEY FACTOR IN IMPLEMENTING YOUR DESIGN (OR GETTING PERMISSION DO SO).

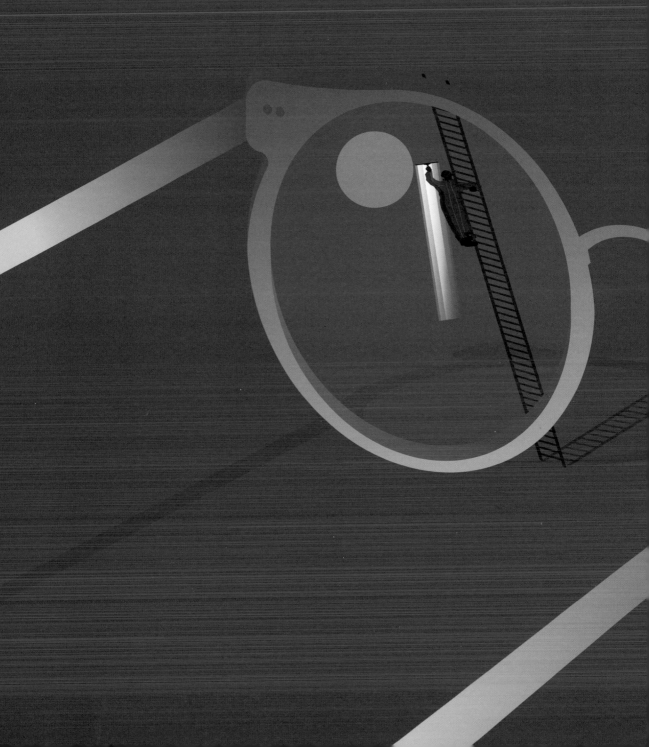

UATE

EVALUATE

The final stage is **EVALUATE**. Here, it is determined whether the intent and associated outcomes (as discussed in the **INTENT**) have been achieved. Evaluation requires an understanding of the quantitative and qualitative metrics of success: the measurements assessed to establish whether the design has accomplished what was intended. It is best to determine these metrics prior to reaching evaluations (that way they can act as a target).

Metrics are often quantitative in nature as most businesses prefer to rely on large data sets and statistics to back financial investments and calculate the return on the investment. However, it is important to also consider qualitative metrics to evaluate the design in more intangible ways. This is also useful to understand and gain insights on how the solution may need to evolve to ensure emerging challenges or potential opportunities are not missed. After all, design is iterative. The risk of resting on a successful evaluation is dangerous for a company. The most successful organisations are those who are constantly aiming to improve on the latest success. Looking forward is key and going back to the first two components (**CONSIDER** and **AUDIT**) can help you anticipate new competitors, market trends and customer needs – allowing you to stay ahead of the curve.

The hardest part of the evaluation phase is determining what success looks like for the organisation. Many organisations will suggest a healthier bank balance here, making it an equation on the return of the investment. Or perhaps it is the continuation and survival of the firm through disruptive times? Either way, this evaluation can be done through traditional metrics and financial means.[7]

But what about the customer and the evaluation of their overall investment in your solution? Or the value placed on the emotional relationship you have built by better understanding their needs – which may be utilised in other services or products? The value of knowing your customers and the difference you make to their lives is difficult to measure and

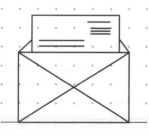

[7] As designers, finance isn't our bread and butter. We need to be able to get across it (understand it) – but there will usually be financial wizards and other experts to help.

therefore evaluate. Practicing design innovation may require you to look at how you evaluate in a different way.

Key questions to ask during this stage are what the impact of your solution will be:
- ✕ WITHIN THE COMPANY?
- ✕ WITHIN THE MARKET?
- ✕ FOR THE CUSTOMER?
- ✕ ENVIRONMENTALLY?
- ✕ ON SOCIETY?

For this component ensuring the unbiased appraisal of the solution is vital, one such approach is to involve multiple stakeholders to overcome any potential bias. While customer satisfaction is the typical focus when assessing a solution, key learnings (insights) from the design and its overall value should also be considered as measures of success. These might be more difficult to prove, and substantial pre-planning should be done to ensure the larger picture (not only the solution in isolation) is taken into account; determine how your solution and work will be evaluated as early as possible. In keeping with traditional methods of evaluation, we believe **METRICS** to be the core aspect of **EVALUATE**. No tools are provided for this component, as evaluation is extremely dependent on your design and context. In the spirit of the book, we'd like you to figure this one out for yourselves. If you're looking for direction we'd recommend doing some reading on traditional market research.

METRICS

CORE **METRICS**

So, your project has come to an end or your design has been launched. It's time to **EVALUATE** your efforts. One way of doing this is by measuring metrics. Not any metrics mind you, it has to be the right ones. Metrics are common practice and essential for a successful business to operate. For instance, most people work every day to achieve key performance indicators (KPIs) set by management. These are just one form of measurement for success. Regardless of specific metrics or measurement, the main question of metrics is: 'did we achieve what we set out to be achieved in the first place?' (the **INTENT**)

Before we get to asking that, we should first ask:
X WHO DECIDES WHAT IS SUCCESSFUL?
X WHAT ARE THE CURRENT METRICS USED?
X HOW ARE THINGS MEASURED?
X WHEN ARE METRICS OF SUCCESS CONSIDERED AND SET?
X HOW OFTEN AND FOR HOW LONG ARE THEY MEASURED?
X ARE THERE ANY SET REQUIREMENTS AROUND METRICS FOR A PROJECT?

The kinds of metrics used vary from traditional financial means to value-based customer offerings. The important thing to know is what to measure and how to measure it. For instance, if you are being realistic then a small project should only be expected to have a limited impact. This kind of expectation should be acknowledged early in the project. Sometimes a small change in perception is required for people to understand and value the impact or success of a project. For important decision makers in the organisation, a shift in their perception surrounding the customer could have significant effects on the organisation's future direction. Success in a small pilot project can also pave the way for bigger projects in the future. This list is certainly not exhaustive, but you can usually measure design across a project, a product and a service (Buchanan, 2001). We also explore how it can be

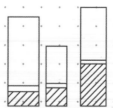

integrated and measured within an organisation in the next part of the book.

Unfortunately, we can't cover every type of metric for every type of design, there are simply too many. However, we can paint a broad picture of what you are looking for in terms of metrics in a number of contexts. For instance, at a project level you can look at metrics pertaining to the:

✕ SCHEDULE (DID THE PROJECT RUN OVER TIME?)
✕ COSTS (DID THE PROJECT COME IN UNDER BUDGET?)
✕ QUALITY (DID THE FINAL OUTCOME PRODUCE QUALITY
   MANUFACTURING IN ITS FINAL FORM?)

These are all performance related metrics that can be tied to a business case.

At a product level you might look at how disruptive the product was in the marketplace. For example; Assink's (2006) work on incremental to radical product placements and the corresponding level of risk to an organisation. Questions to ask include:

✕ HOW DISRUPTIVE OF AN INNOVATION DID YOU CREATE?
✕ WHAT WAS THE ORGANISATION LOOKING FOR?
✕ DID YOU SET OUT TO DEVELOP A NEW TECHNOLOGY
   AND DISRUPT THE TECHNOLOGY RADICALLY?

Other methods for evaluating product success include traditional market research, which could entail measuring customer satisfaction across criteria like aesthetics, brand value, emotional affect and functionality (Moultrie, Clarkson & Probert, 2006). This could be done through a scorecard that numerically or emotively measures criteria that are valued by the organisation on a scale ranging from poor- to good-performance. Preferably, these criteria would pre-determined, so that there are no unwanted surprises.

No two products, services or projects are the same – so finding the right metrics to measure can be challenging. Nevertheless, there are plenty of resources available to help you determine the right metrics, and your organisation and colleagues are first amongst these. Remember to not leave evaluation to the last minute. Establishing metrics early on is essential for ensuring that your output will meet the right criteria.

DRIVING QUESTIONS

EVALUATE

What does success look like within the company, within the marketplace and for the customer?
- ✕ *How will you measure success or failure?*

What is the impact of your solution:
- ✕ *Within the company?*
- ✕ *Within the market?*
- ✕ *For the customer?*
- ✕ *Environmentally?*
- ✕ *On society?*

Who in the organisation decides if your project was a success?
- ✕ *How will they establish this?*

What are the current metrics used for determining the success of a project?
- ✕ *How often and for how long are they measured?*
- ✕ *Are there any set requirements around metrics for a project?*

What have you learnt from this process?
- ✕ *Has this process made you look at your innovation process differently? If yes, how so?*

If your company requires a change in business model configuration, how will you start this process of change?
- ✕ *What is required and how much change is required?*

SUMMARY

In the first part of the book we:

✗ EXPLAINED THE ORIGINS AND EVOLUTIONS OF DESIGN

✗ STEPPED OUT THE NON-LINEAR STRUCTURE AND SIX COMPONENTS OF THE DESIGN INNOVATION FRAMEWORK

✗ ELABORATED ON THE CORE ASPECT OF EACH COMPONENT IN THE FRAMEWORK

✗ INTRODUCED TOOLS AND KEY DRIVING QUESTIONS TO HELP GUIDE YOU THROUGH EACH OF THE COMPONENTS.

As we discussed earlier, our framework is a cognitive approach of conscious and considered actions and choices. There is no recipe (design is not a secret sauce, though maybe Aioli could be?) or a 'correct' way of applying it. You will need to consider what you need next in your project and oscillate between the components as necessary – constantly moving back and forth as required by the project. Once you have mastered this you should begin to think how the components can be redesigned to better suit your purpose. A cookie-cutter approach will never be as good as one that is tailored to the practitioner and the project.

The components, core aspects, and example tools and methods (blank templates included at the back) are your signposts for design. We hope that they inspire your design endeavours, and that they empower you to experiment, be bold and think critically. Remember that design is not a prescriptive checklist. Do not limit your approach to what has been written in this book and other texts.

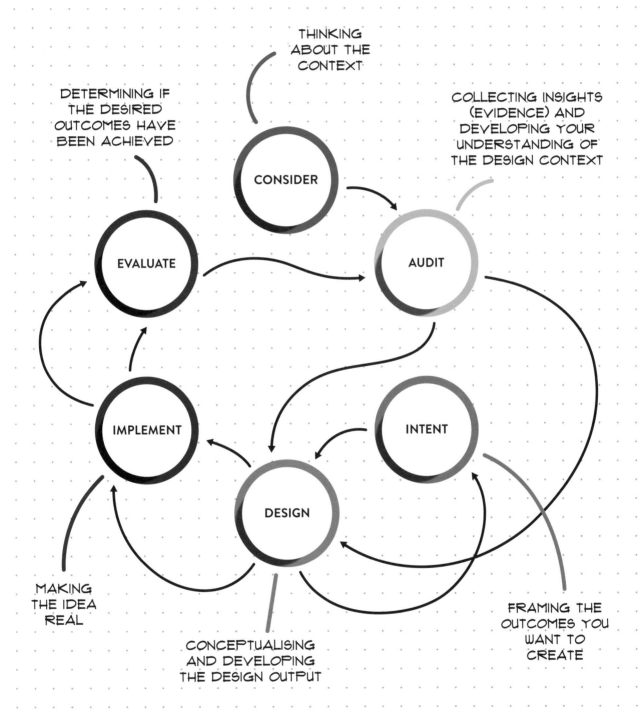

THINKING
ABOUT THE
CONTEXT

DETERMINING IF
THE DESIRED
OUTCOMES HAVE
BEEN ACHIEVED

COLLECTING INSIGHTS
(EVIDENCE) AND
DEVELOPING YOUR
UNDERSTANDING OF
THE DESIGN CONTEXT

CONSIDER

EVALUATE

AUDIT

IMPLEMENT

INTENT

DESIGN

MAKING
THE IDEA
REAL

FRAMING THE
OUTCOMES YOU
WANT TO
CREATE

CONCEPTUALISING
AND DEVELOPING
THE DESIGN OUTPUT

DESIGN INTEGRATION

In the first part of this book we explained design innovation and discussed the six components:

✕ CONSIDER
✕ AUDIT
✕ INTENT
✕ DESIGN
✕ IMPLEMENT
✕ EVALUATE.

We also focused on design as a means of conceiving an output such as a product, service, system or business model. However, this is not always the full intent and sole objective of design. Beyond the tangible outputs of design (such as those described before), designers can also be concerned with the future of design in the organisation in which design is being practised. This aspect is to do with design integration, which we refer to as the process of embedding design as a strategic resource across all facets of an organisation. It is not a separate objective and should (if implemented correctly) align to design work that is already occurring (for instance in a project). Design integration can follow the same components as outlined in the first part of this book, but with a focus on creating the ideal conditions for the continued use of design across different facets of an organisation. We cover four concepts which are key to design integration:

✕ DESIGN CATALYST
✕ ORGANISATIONAL CONDITIONS
✕ THINKING STYLES
✕ DESIGN PRINCIPLES.

Design leaders seeking to undertake design integration within their organisations are provided with a process to follow and tips to overcome potential challenges. In this part of the book, the role of the **DESIGN CATALYST** is explicated. The four **ORGANISATIONAL CONDITIONS** required for design integration are detailed and explained so the reader can easily

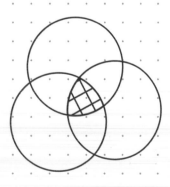

identify design's relationship to the strategic aspects of an organisation. Different **THINKING STYLES** are examined, to demonstrate the outcomes of the different approaches and how each style can be utilised throughout different stages of a project. **DESIGN PRINCIPLES** are then shared to illustrate typical hurdles in design integration and how these can be overcome. Key takeaways are also included at the end of each section to allow for quick reference to what was covered.

Design can be the foundation of a competitive advantage when integrated within an organisation (Wrigley, Nusem & Straker, 2020). If this were an easy process, then everyone would be doing it. One popular approach for realising design integration is through a series of design projects or engagements that seek to tackle isolated or congruent opportunities and challenges – otherwise known as design interventions. Regrettably, few design interventions result in design integration.

We can tell you from our experience that the process of translating a once-off activity (a design intervention) into a permanent repeatable practice (design integration) is complex. Nevertheless, design interventions can (Wrigley, Nusem & Straker, 2020):

✗ demonstrate and develop an awareness of design's value through smaller, more manageable projects
✗ generate interest in design and create a desire for design
✗ guide design action within an organisation.

For these reasons, a design intervention can be considered to play a critical role in the integration of design. The impact of subsequent design interventions can be considered as cumulative, with each intervention serving to create awareness of, interest in, and desire for design (Nusem, Matthews & Wrigley, 2019). Ultimately, these phases result in design action, which is a requisite of integration. Indeed, design interventions can help get the organisation closer to integration. An organisation that widely implements design (through its staff) and recognises design as a strategic asset can be considered to have achieved design integration. Keep in mind that design integration requires more than an understanding of design. It requires an organisational appetite for design and the capacity to use it.

FROM INTERVENTION TO INTEGRATION

GN CATALYST

DESIGN CATALYST

A DC IS A DESIGNER WHO LEADS DESIGN INTERVENTIONS WITH THE AIM OF INTEGRATING DESIGN WITHIN AN ORGANISATION.

As discussed earlier in the book the field of design innovation is positioned at the intersection of design, innovation and business, and thus serves as a viable tool for guiding strategy (Martin, 2007). Navigating the nexus of these disciplines requires a unique skillset, and individuals that do so are able to act as catalysts for change inside organisations (Norman, 2010). Demand for such individuals has grown over the years alongside the acceptance of design thinking in education and practice. Much of our work has been about understanding how the specific knowledge and skills of a designer can be better articulated, understood, implemented and valued as a core component of strategy and innovation in business (Wrigley, 2016). The Design Catalyst (DC) was born out of this line of inquiry. They are a valuable asset for managing business and design knowledge domains and are usually the ones responsible for driving a design intervention within an organisation.

This is not to say that all designers need to be across both of these domains (over to the dark side as some purists would say), but rather that this emerging field needs to be better understood. There will always be the need for professional disciplinary designers in addition to, not in the place of, these new-generation hybrids.

The DC's role is to translate and facilitate design observation, insight, meaning, and strategy across all facets of an organisation (Krippendorff, 1989). A DC is a designer who leads design interventions with the aim of integrating design within an organisation. Early, continued stakeholder engagement and buy-in are an essential part of this, as by nature the insights sought by the catalyst generate discussion, debate, and perhaps controversy to challenge the way things have always been done. Based on the authors' research and first-hand experiences, the DC's general capabilities were conceived (Wrigley, 2016).

The DC has a unique set of six capabilities essential for the implementation of design innovation:

1. Designer Intuition
2. Business Acumen
3. Agile Facilitation
4. Customer Centred
5. Rule Breaker
6. Research Rigour

DESIGN INTUITION

Inherent design knowledge and skills are integral parts of the catalyst's role. One key design skill is visualisation, which can enable fluid communication between the various disciplines/departments in an organisation. A designer's skills and knowledge also assist with problem-solving, facilitation, and content generation. Lacking these skills would result in a catalyst who is only capable of capturing a record of what is being voiced in the project. They would likely be unable to shape content, engage the audience, and facilitate meaningful participation. Designers also have trust in the design journey over the outcome, which can present a major conflict in risk-averse organisations that may insist on a pre-determined design outcome. These are difficult skills to learn on the fly, so we recommend some sort of prior design training or qualification. The key capabilities you should focus on developing are:

X DESIGN VISUALISATION SKILLS (TO ENABLE COMMUNICATION BETWEEN THE VARIOUS DEPARTMENTS IN A FIRM)

X COMFORT WITH AMBIGUITY (DESIGN CAN BE QUITE UNCERTAIN, BUT THIS IS NOT AN EXCUSE FOR POOR PROJECT MANAGEMENT)

X ABILITY TO FACILITATE A DESIGN ENABLED CONVERSATION USING VISUAL ILLUSTRATION METHODS AND MEANS

X AGILITY TO SCAFFOLD DESIGN PRACTICE AS REQUIRED BY THE PROJECT

BUSINESS ACUMEN

A basic understanding of key business theory and application concepts (e.g. strategy, business models, new product development, organisational change, entrepreneurship, innovation, marketing, etc.) are all required by the DC. Some of these concepts can be learned in formal design education, but many represent knowledge from other disciplines. Much of this knowledge is gained through professional or practical experience throughout. For instance, while working as an in-house designer or in a consultancy. A basic understanding of business processes (such as the development of products and services) allows the DC to participate in conversations regarding the drivers of the business. It also assists in the use of design innovation when solving an organisation's more complex business problems. Key capabilities include:

X KNOWLEDGE AND UNDERSTANDING OF BUSINESS'S STRATEGY, NEW PRODUCT DEVELOPMENT, INCREMENTAL TO RADICAL INNOVATION, ORGANISATIONAL CHANGE, AND ENTREPRENEURIAL AWARENESS

X THE ABILITY TO PARTICIPATE IN BUSINESS DISCOURSE USED COMMONLY BY THE ORGANISATION AND INDUSTRY

X USING DESIGN TO CROSS HERETICAL BOUNDARIES WHEN IDENTIFYING KEY DRIVERS FOR FUTURE GROWTH

X LEVERAGING DIFFERENT THINKING STYLES TO CHALLENGE THE ESTABLISHED ASSUMPTIONS HELD IN THE BUSINESS

X AN UNDERSTANDING OF BUSINESS MODEL CONCEPTS AND HOW THESE ELEMENTS ARE STRUCTURED IN DIFFERENT INDUSTRIES.

AGILE FACILITATION

The ability to think independently, originally and outside the box (inherent to designers) are paramount in a DC. They will also be able to appreciate other ways of thinking and should strive for cognitive diversity in their work. This allows them to employ creative, collaborative problem-solving skills across the organisation. The ability to envisage and understand multifaceted, complex problems from multiple perspectives, and manoeuvre around constraints are also necessities. Cognitive abilities are a difficult skill to master but will naturally develop alongside your experience and the mistakes you make (and learn from). DCs are capable of translating ideas from the abstract to the concrete realm, as we have established earlier in the book (in DESIGN). They are also able to re-frame problems and align the value proposition of a given idea to the organisation's strategy. Key capabilities include the ability to:

X THINK CREATIVELY, INDEPENDENTLY, AND ORIGINALLY

X COLLABORATE WITH OTHERS TO ENCOURAGE IDEAS AND EMPLOY CREATIVE PROBLEM-SOLVING SKILLS

X RAPIDLY TRANSLATE IDEAS THROUGH PROTOTYPING

INTO REAL CONCEPTS
× RE-FRAME PROBLEMS SPONTANEOUSLY (THIS
   REQUIRES SOME MASTERY)
× COMFORTABLY 'KILL' AN IDEA IF IT DOESN'T ALIGN TO
   THE ORGANISATION'S STRATEGY
× BE ADAPTABLE AND CAPABLE OF CONVERGING AND
   DIVERGING QUICKLY
× CHALLENGE THE FUNDAMENTAL PROBLEMS AND
   CONSTRAINTS INVOLVED WITH A PROJECT.

CUSTOMER CENTRED

While design practice is inherently customer-centric, organisations can quickly lose sight of the customer in the internal processes and politics of bringing a product to market (Moore, 1999). The DC's role is to uncover customers' latent needs and values (as discussed in AUDIT) and to synthesise these into insights that can be presented to the organisation. Ideally, these insights should be brought to the attention of the senior executives, the leadership or management teams, or whoever makes decisions about future products or services. DCs are well placed to collect customer insights due to their empathy, which is a core practice of a designer's training. Their ability to build genuine emotional connections with customers and other stakeholders is a vital part of ensuring that a design is desired. They are also able to manage and balance the often conflicting interests of stakeholders. Being customer and stakeholder centred provides the ability to:

× OBJECTIVELY EMPATHISE WITH CUSTOMERS AND
   STAKEHOLDER ISSUES WITHOUT BIAS
× DEVELOP A SHARED UNDERSTANDING OF A
   COMPANY'S VISION WITH STAKEHOLDERS.
× GROW GENUINE EMOTIONAL CONNECTIONS WITH
   STAKEHOLDERS
× COLLABORATE AND ENGAGE WITH STAKEHOLDERS
   THROUGH DESIGN PRACTICE.

RULE BREAKER

Personality is important in most facilitation roles as it can help to stimulate engagement across different groups of people. This can help to draw out rich information that encourages and inspires others to get involved. People are not always forthcoming with information – being personable can help build rapport and a safe environment for people to share their thoughts and ideas. The DC navigates and then facilitates future orientated scenarios such as disruptive markets, burning platforms (a product offering that is no longer desirable), and family conflicts (in family-owned businesses); in some situations, the personal capabilities of the DC become vital. An open mind and perpetual optimism are needed to reframe problems into opportunities for organisations, especially during large industry downturns (...or global pandemics). Personal qualities help the designer to:

✕ STIMULATE, PROVOKE, ENCOURAGE, INSPIRE AND MOTIVATE OTHERS INSIDE AN ORGANISATION
✕ FACILITATE COMPLEX CHALLENGES
✕ HAVE A HOLISTIC VIEW OF THE ORGANISATION AND BE IMPARTIAL
✕ PRESENT A CHEERFUL AND ENTHUSIASTIC PERSONA AS WELL AS AN AUTHENTIC DRIVE TO LEARN (NO ONE PERSON HOLDS THE ANSWERS, IT'S A TEAM EFFORT)
✕ BE OPEN-MINDED AND OPTIMISTIC.

RESEARCH RIGOUR

The DC cannot be seen to have all the answers, and nor should they. If they do, then they are likely making assumptions. Everything needs to be grounded in research, with a focus on both the internal and external aspects of the organisation (as we discussed in **CONSIDER** and **AUDIT**). This groundwork allows the DC to speak from a position of unbiased authority, to rely on data (the voice of the customer or other stakeholders rather than their own opinions), and to channel the voice of employees (for instance, through a reverse persona as discussed in design tools). The DC presents the evidence (research) and then facilitates design practice with relevant stakeholders to address the problem or opportunity at hand. They investigate, gather, absorb, and analyse data independently, as well as collectively, to present a solution to the business. Figuring out how to conduct research and what type of research is appropriate can be tricky, and usually requires some form of formal research training. Research knowledge and skills include:

✕ THE ABILITY TO SOURCE RIGOROUS, RELEVANT KNOWLEDGE
✕ BEING ABLE TO UNDERSTAND, CRITIQUE, AND SYNTHESISE FINDINGS INTO USEFUL APPLICATIONS FOR AN ORGANISATION
✕ CAPACITY TO PRESENT RESEARCH IN AN UNBIASED AND ETHICAL FASHION
✕ THE APTITUDE TO GENERATE RESULTS, REFLECT ON FINDINGS AND DISSEMINATE NEW KNOWLEDGE.

A DC – through their knowledge, skills, and an understanding of stakeholders and context – can facilitate innovation and assist organisations to remain relevant. Catalysts see themselves as disseminators of knowledge that help companies navigate economic uncertainty and organisational politics. Regardless of their capabilities, a DC requires support from the organisation to properly execute their role. This might be from the head of a department who is championing design, or it could be buy-in from the organisation's executive team. Without support, the DC is unlikely to have access to the people and resources required for design innovation. The **DESIGN CATALYST CANVAS** can be used to illuminate your own key skills and characteristics while such capabilities can be assessed and benchmarked against in the **DESIGN CATALYST CAPABILITIES** tool.

A DC is a valuable asset to any organisation due to their specialised knowledge, tools, processes and capacity to demonstrate the value of design. They are known as knowledge disseminators, change catalysts and organisational culture reformists in the industry. A large part of their value offering is their ability to identify and understand the future and latent needs of current or prospective customers. Another added value is the way they plan, orchestrate and execute change, allowing for organic cultural shifts to occur and for organisations to leverage new designs and innovation opportunities.

- ✗ Invest in quality design cognate staff – if possible (accredited) trained designers (a good way to evaluate this is with the **DESIGN CATALYSTS CAPABILITIES** template in the back of this book)
- ✗ A DC should be hired from outside the organisation (an internal worker will likely struggle to dissociate from their previous role and existing workstreams)
- ✗ Give them the space, permission, and remit to work autonomously.
- ✗ Allow their work to be directed by customer needs and values.
- ✗ Be lenient with descriptors for key performance indicators (design practice is uncertain, overly specific performance metrics can stifle creativity and the outcomes/outputs of design)
- ✗ Provide a political umbrella for their work so it can span across departments and get the traction it requires.

VALUE OF THE DESIGN CATALYST

TAKEAWAYS FOR DC BOSSES

DESIGN CATALYST CAPABILITIES are a combination of underlying skills, knowledge and abilities of a Design Catalyst and consist of:

CUSTOMER CENTRED:
ability to put the customer first and empathise with their latent needs.

RESEARCH RIGOR:
ability to source relevant knowledge, to understand, investigate, synthesise, critique such findings into useful applications in the organisation.

DESIGN INTUITION:
ability to visualise, translate ideas, prototype concepts, understand the design process and be able to apply it instinctively, without the need for conscious reasoning.

AGILE FACILITATION:
ability to stimulate, provoke, encourage, inspire, motivate others, lead through example, and experiment collaboratively.

BUSINESS ACUMEN:
foundational knowledge including but not exclusively; strategy, new product development, incremental/radical innovation, business model innovation, customer relationships, marketing, organisational change and entrepreneurial awareness.

RULE BREAKER:
Ability to challenge the status quo, beliefs, product problems and constraints, procedural processes, assumptions and to re-frame problems.

This tool can be used to rank your design innovation capabilities. To fill it out, decide how confident you are with each of the capabilities on a scale of 1-5 (1 being weak and 5 being strong), and draw a line between each of the dimensions as shown below. This will help you determine which areas you could improve in.

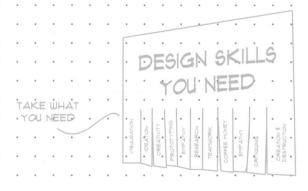

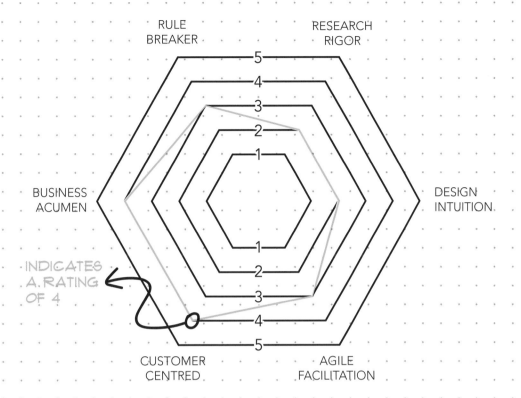

The **DESIGN CATALYST** can assist to assess an individual for the characteristics and skillsets required in a DC (i.e. a designer who leads design interventions with the aim of integrating design within an organisation). This Tool can be used to asses, hire, benchmark, train or appoint a Design Catalyst, and to determine what value a DC provides to an organisation (and how).

You can use this tool in two different ways.
1. If you are an organisation looking to appoint a DC: you can use this to prompt questions in a job interview that explore more than where the candidate recently worked and for how long. It will allow you to probe into the desired personality traits and underlying skills needed by a designer (you will obviously still need to ask all the other questions that HR love to ask). Additionally, it can help you craft your job advertisement, so that can attract the right candidates in the first place.

2. If you have DC aspirations or already acting in this role: you can use this tool to honestly answer where you are strongest and identify areas where you could use improvement or development. Use the template **DESIGN CATALYST** and begin to work your way through the questions. Do not use one-word answers, attempt to provide as much detail as possible (not just the obvious response).

DESIGN CATALYST EXAMPLE

Paul is a DC who has been working in a company (even though his job title is brand strategist). He is trying to position himself more in the innovation portfolio inside the company and be more proactive in driving innovation efforts inside the firm. He decides to complete the **DESIGN CATALYST** to see where he can improve his skills in order to do this.

HELPERS

Who helps you provide and deliver this value?

X LINKS INTO THE SALES TEAM (SO I CAN GAIN ACCESS TO CUSTOMERS)

X INDUSTRY NETWORK – LATEST IN BRANDING EVENTS

X GET IN FRONT OF THE CUSTOMER MYSELF

X NETWORK/MEET UP WITH OTHERS FROM MY UNIVERSITY ALUMNI WHO ARE DOING THIS NOW IN VARIOUS ORGANISATIONS FOR SUPPORT

CAN EXPAND THIS! CONNECT WITH MORE PEOPLE ON LINKEDLIN

ACTIONS

What you do on a daily basis to reinforce your value?

X DESIGN VISUALISATION

X GENERATE INSIGHTS (FROM SECONDARY DATA)

X TEACH THE INTERNAL STAKEHOLDERS ABOUT THE BRAND

X CHALLENGE ASSUMPTIONS MORE

CHARACTERISTICS

Who are you and what makes you different?

X CURIOUS TO LEARN DRIVE TO INNOVATE

X WANT TO TRY NEW THINGS PASSIONATE ABOUT THE COMPANY

X DON'T ACCEPT THINGS THAT WAY THEY ARE JUST BECAUSE THIS IS HOW THEY HAVE ALWAYS BEEN DONE

NEED TO IMPROVE!!

CATALYST VALUE

SKILLS

DELIVERY

How do you help?

× BRAND IDENTITY &
STRATEGY

× COMPANY VISION
ROADMAP FORWARD TO
COMPANY

× GOOD KNOWLEDGE OF
CUSTOMER INSIGHTS

× DESIGNING BUSINESS
MODELS

× LINKS TO UNITED
INNOVATION EFFORTS ACROSS
THE ORGANISATION

× SEAT AT THE TABLE TO
TALK AND BE TAKEN
SERIOUSLY IN REGARDS TO
COMPANY STRATEGY

What expertise do you require?

× VISUAL GRAPHIC DESIGN

× CUSTOMER JOURNEY MAPS
PERSONAS

× ABILITY TO VIEW
PROBLEMS FORM THE
CUSTOMER PERSPECTIVE

× INTERPERSONAL SKILLS
CO-DESIGN SKILLS
LEADERSHIP

INSTRUMENTS

How do you deliver value?

× INTERNAL NETWORKS

× GOOD INDUSTRY NETWORKS

× GROUP FACILITATION INTERNAL
& EXTERNAL

× INDUSTRY STANDARDS

Who do you help?

× THE MARKETING &
COMMUNICATIONS DEPARTMENT

× THE PROJECT TEAMS

× CUSTOMERS

× C-SUITE OF THE FIRM
PROJECT LEADERS

ORGANISATIONAL CONDITIONS

ORGANISATIONAL CONDITIONS

Organisations have their own sets of rules, practices and shared understandings, and are typically the platform through which design is practiced. Naturally, for design integration to achieve optimal outcomes in such arrangements, the right conditions need to be present – or at least considered (as previously explained in **CONSIDER**). The four conditions are (Wrigley, Nusem & Straker, 2020):

1. strategic vision – the organisation's long-term strategic goals and intent that include incorporating design
2. facilities – resources and spaces dedicated to design activities
3. cultural capital – an understanding of design and its value, and a capacity to practice it in the organisation's workforce
4. directive(s) – mandate(s) that call for the use of design and hold the organisation's staff accountable to use design.

Each of these conditions influences the uptake of design within an organisation, and collectively they frame how much support design is given. If the conditions are not established in an organisation, a design practitioner may find it difficult to conduct the activities required in a holistic design practice, or to get the traction required to invest in a new design opportunity. Indeed, sometimes the focus of design is on establishing these conditions rather on an actual design output, so that a future for design in the organisation can be established. These conditions are further detailed in the following sections.

STRATEGIC VISION

Strategic vision refers to the organisation's long-term intent, plan or direction, and is often captured in through a mission statement or value proposition (Wrigley, Nusem & Straker, 2020). In essence, it defines what the organisation could and should be in the future – both in terms of its aspirations and what it should represent (Ian, 1992). Internally, an organisation's vision inspires and motivates its people, while externally a vision differentiates an organisation from its competitors (Coulson-Thomas, 1992). A vision, like any other organisational construct, is influenced by a myriad of factors including risk aversion, appetite for change, growth and innovation, and a capacity to balance existing and future business horizons.

A well-defined strategic vision can assist an organisation to pursue the right goals and is a source of competitiveness. Conversely, an organisation without vision is unlikely to lead, and will often need to respond to market trends rather than define them (Wrigley, Nusem & Straker, 2020). A good vision is one that is coherent, powerful, achievable, and aspirational, describes the future focus of the organisation, and establishes what success looks like (Ian, 1992).

You can define a strategic vision in four general steps (Schoemaker, 1992):

1. Generate a broad range of future scenarios that the organisation may encounter.
2. Analyse the organisation's industry and the strategic segments therein (thus grasping the organisation's position within the market).
3. Understand the organisation and its competitors' core capabilities, so as to understand the sustainability of a proposed strategic vision (and its potential to be replicated by competitors).
4. Identify the strategic options available to the organisation and establish a strategic vision.

The role of the individual is also pivotal in establishing a strategic vision for an organisation. Senior managers should not be the only parties with a role in shaping an organisation's vision, and dialogue with an organisation's people that promotes both intrinsic and extrinsic motivations for a vision can help ensure it's appropriate (Hodgkinson, 2002). A vision that is blind to the organisation's people, and the internal or external environment is one that is likely to fail. It is also important to remember that people and markets change – and so too must the organisation evolve and adapt. Setting a strategic vision is an ongoing process; this is not a 'set and forget' activity (Hodgkinson, 2002).

FACILITIES

Facilities capture the spaces and resources, both physical and digital, that are available for design in an organisation. A physical location for design (like a design hub, war room, or project room) is a critical factor in the success of design (Leifer & Steinert, 2011). Design, lacking such a space, is unlikely to get much traction – staff will presume that it is not supported or a key priority. It is not only about fitting design into the current organisational structures, but also about changing practices in the organisation to support design. Broadly speaking, facilities refer to the organisation facilitating design activities.

Design requires proper facilities to function as intended, especially in the long-term. If you want to go beyond temporary engagements that promote short-term outcomes, then making sure that staff are properly equipped to tackle design and have the spaces (and therefore capacity) to bring the rest of the organisation along for the journey is integral. We've broken these needs down to two primary components: physical spaces and resources.

The role of a physical space is vital. From a practical perspective, it provides the organisation's people a space (e.g. a meeting room) in which to practise design, ensuring that they have access to what they need when it is needed. A physical space also:

✗ DEMONSTRATES THE ORGANISATION'S SUPPORT FOR THE INITIATIVE
✗ PROVIDES TRANSPARENCY OVER WHAT DESIGN WORK IS HAPPENING (IF SET UP CORRECTLY)
✗ CAN BE A GREAT WAY TO GENERATE HYPE ABOUT ACTIVITIES AND OUTCOMES EMERGING FROM DESIGN PRACTICE.

Like any other activity, design needs to be properly resourced for its outputs to be of value. Just as a construction worker would not be able to renovate your home without access to the tools required for the job, it would be ill-advised to instigate design work without the designer having access to what they require. Resources can include the physical things required to design (e.g. basic stationery and prototyping materials), specialist software (such as that required to create models or compelling graphics for a project), and/or support in accessing the right stakeholders (e.g. incentives for participants in focus groups or interviews, or some time with a busy executive to give feedback on a concept or design).

Cultural capital is about an organisation's people, whether they understand the value of design, and if they are capable of practising design. Organisations tend to underinvest in the development and management of their people, as this has traditionally been seen as a diversion of profit (Pickett, 2005). However, an organisation's human resources are integral to its success (Wright & Mcmahan, 2011). These resources represent an organisation's capacity to achieve its goals and are a key asset in conceiving such goals.

Realising design practice in an organisation isn't just about the goal. The organisation's people need to understand why design should be used and valued, and how they could use it. This can be achieved through training – formal or otherwise – that provides people the skills they need to practise design. Recognising the value of design is less tangible and straightforward. It requires that the organisation's people have seen what design can achieve, either through a previous, successfully implemented design or through a promising ongoing project within the organisation. This can be done through a combination of pilot studies and projects (which demonstrate the value), and workshops (that teach the key skills) – i.e., through any sort of design intervention.

Building the skills required can be tricky, but it is also just one component of establishing capability in the workforce. Unlike investments made in something concrete like real estate, an organisation's workforce is subject to fluctuation — it is inevitable that people come and go. This presents a key risk and is a strong argument for why organisations should focus on retention. Otherwise, your knowledge can simply walk out the door (Leonard & Sensiper, 1998). Without the know-how, an innovation project cannot progress. A large component that influences retention is an organisation's culture. This not only contributes to the extent to which innovation and creativity occur (Martins & Terblanche, 2003), but is a key determinant of retention (Chatterjee, 2009).

Directives, in this context, imply a mandate for design practice within an organisation. This mandate can take many forms but is generally communicated through Key Performance

CULTURAL CAPITAL

DIRECTIVE(S)

Indicators (KPIs) in private organisations, or through legislation in government or non-profit entities. Having a mandate is the first step, closely followed by building accountability for following the mandate and by aligning general practice to the mandate. In large organisations general practice is changed by altering the processes through which practice is done (Dearlove, 2006). This requires clear directive(s) to be set, as most individuals won't go out of their way to do something that isn't encouraged, requested or known. Making sure that the organisation's goals are met requires clear communication surrounding what those goals are.

Directives guide staff to act in a way that aligns with an organisation's vision and provides a form of accountability for staff (so that the desired actions are known). The intent is not to create a rigid bureaucracy, but to inform people that design is part of their role. KPIs can be used to accomplish this, as they offer a structured way of sharing and building expectations and a formal reporting structure for establishing whether those expectations have been met. Another notable method is through strategic incentives for outcomes emerging from employee's actions. For example, through awards and recognition by external bodies, or through celebrations and promotion within the organisation for achieving or meeting key milestones.

THE FRAMEWORKS

Now that we have covered the theory of the organisational conditions we can begin to unpack how they can be applied in practice. As we describe earlier in the book, there is no one tool or approach for solving any given problem. In fact, many of the tools and frameworks we describe could (if modified appropriately) be suitable for assisting with multiple components in the design innovation framework. A persona, for example, is listed as a tool for auditing, but could easily be used to frame intent for a design through a descriptive, salient quote. e.g. "I love the auto-top up features on my public transport access card, but it makes it difficult to track my spending". A manager or reverse persona (as discussed when introducing design tools) can be useful in the consider and implement components, as they provide a way to understand who could champion design and a means for communicating with an organisation respectively. The organisational conditions are no different and have a myriad of applications. We describe three such applications, with the last two described in additional detail in the following sections:

1. a framework used to understand the current state of each of the conditions in an organisation (this was discussed earlier in the book we talked about the 'consider' component of the framework, see pg.58).
2. an audit for gauging alignment between front-line and executive staff across each of the conditions.
3. a matrix for conceptualising how each of the conditions could be improved, and how each condition could be leveraged to improve or align to another.

The **ORGANISATIONAL CONDITIONS AUDIT** was conceived for an external party (such as an external consultant with limited knowledge of an organisation)[8] to get their bearings in relation to the current state of the organisational conditions. Unlike the other two iterations which could be largely filled out based on subject matter expert's inherent knowledge, this iteration requires the user to collect some data. This might be formally acquired through some interviews with front-line staff and members of the executive team, or through informal breakout room conversations with an agenda. Ultimately, in this form the user is able to explore existing perspectives and knowledge about the organisational conditions from front-line and executive perspectives. The goal is to consider whether these perspectives are aligned, or if there are differences between what has been conceived by executive and what is known by front-line staff. This can serve to highlight any potential miscommunication (or breakdown in communication) that might have occurred, and can identify which areas an organisation might spend more time developing (both in terms of forming a strategy if there is none, or in better educating and communicating with its staff). For instance, the framework could reveal that executives might be aware of a set of resources available to staff, but that front-line staff are either unaware of these resources or do not know how to effectively access them. Exploring these alignments (or misalignment in this instance) could provide the user with a tangible action they can take to remedy such an issue.

ORGANISATIONAL CONDITIONS AUDIT

[8] We say explicit knowledge of the organisation as it is unlikely that an outsider (that is not intimate with the organisation) will have the knowledge required to meaningfully use this tool. Desktop research could help someone become better acquainted with the organisation, but the subject matter which is critical for this framework is not usually documented online.

ORGANISATIONAL CONDITIONS MATRIX

The **ORGANISATIONAL CONDITIONS MATRIX** was conceptualised to be used by an internal expert (with explicit knowledge of the organisation) to highlight how each of the conditions could be improved, and to assist the user to identify how each of the conditions could be leveraged to improve another. This iteration begins with a brief summary or overview of the questions from the original framework – as it can be quite difficult to understand how to improve something without first knowing its current state – with the user following a set of numbered instructions to complete the framework. After exploring the current state for each individual condition, the user is prompted to think about the potential logic and reasoning behind the current state through a series of questions concerned with the why. The culmination of this process then prompts the user to consider how each of conditions can be leveraged to improve another through their relationships with one-another. Through these guided steps the matrix is able to offer tangible direction(s) for the user to better the state of organisational conditions. Nevertheless, the focus here remains on identification – as significant scoping, buy-in and conceptual development will need to occur prior to the user being able to take an action for improving the conditions.

TAKEAWAYS

✕ THE ORGANISATIONAL CONDITIONS CAN HELP YOU FRAME AN INTERNAL PERSPECTIVE ON AN ORGANISATION IN RELATION TO HOW DESIGN IS USED AND SUPPORTED.

✕ BUILDING OR OPTIMISING THE ORGANISATIONAL CONDITIONS IS REQUIRED FOR AN ORGANISATION THAT IS HOPING TO HAVE A FUTURE FOR DESIGN.

✕ A DESIGN INTERVENTION IS UNLIKELY TO MAKE A LONG-TERM IMPACT WITHOUT THE SUPPORT OF THE ORGANISATIONAL CONDITIONS.

✕ ORGANISATIONAL CONDITIONS CAN BE BUILT ALONGSIDE ONGOING DESIGN ACTIVITY.

✕ NO ONE CONDITION IS IMPORTANT THAN THE OTHERS, BUT THE JOURNEY USUALLY STARTS WITH PUTTING DESIGN ON THE ORGANISATION'S AGENDA (AS PART OF A STRATEGIC VISION).

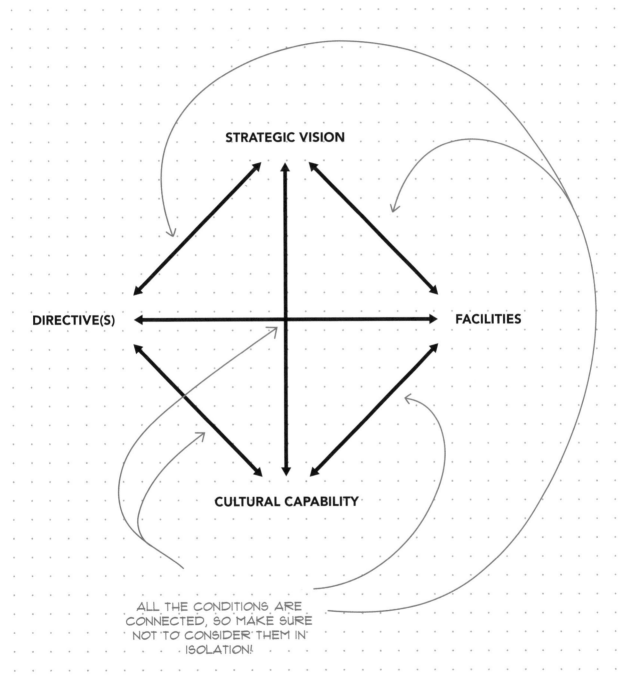

STRATEGIC VISION

DIRECTIVE(S)

FACILITIES

CULTURAL CAPABILITY

ALL THE CONDITIONS ARE CONNECTED, SO MAKE SURE NOT TO CONSIDER THEM IN ISOLATION!

THESE COULD BE COMMUNICATED AS QUOTES, OR AS PARAGRAPH THAT SYNTHESISES WHAT YOU FOUND.

	STRATEGIC VISION	DIRECTIVE(S)
FRONT-LINE	How do front-line staff describe the organisation's vision? What do they think of it? THEY'RE NOT SURE WHAT IT REALLY IS. WHEN ASKED THEY TEND TO DESCRIBE IT AS A SET OF CHARECTERISTICS (OPTIMAL QUALITIES) THEY ASSOCIATE WITH THE BUSINESS (E.G. TRUST AND LOYALTY).	Are the organisation's staff aware of any (non-role specific) design directives(s)? "ACTUALLY, I'M REQUIRED TO DEMONSTRATE MY ABILITY TO CREATIVELY PROBLEM SOLVE. IT'S PROBABLY THE KPI I'M STRESSED MOST ABOUT... NOT REALLY SURE HOW TO DO THAT OR DEMONSTRATE THAT I DID". "UGH, YOU COULD SAY THAT. THE CHIEF CUSTOMER OFFICER TOLD US THAT WE ALL HAVE TO PUT FORWARD SOME SUGGESTIONS ABOUT HOW WE COULD MAKE IS EASIER FOR CUSOMTERS TO ACCOMPLISH THEIR GOALS".
EXECUTIVE	How do the organisation's executive describe its vision? Do they embody this vision? If so, through what actions? "YEAH, WE HAVE A VISION. IT'S WRITTEN ON OUR WEBISTE". THE COMPANY HAS DONE A BRANDING EXERCISE WITH A MARKETING GROUP TO HELP DEFINE A VISION. IT LARGELY SEEMS TO BE FOR THEIR PUBLIC IMAGE THOUGH, RATHER THAN SOMETHING THAT GUIDES THEIR ACTIONS.	What design directives(s) do the organisation's executive team believe staff are following? MEMBERS OF THE EXECUTIVE TEAM ALL SHARED A NUMBER OF METHODS USED TO COMMUNICATE THE ORGANISATION'S DESIGN AGENDA TO STAFF. THESE INCLUDED FORMAL PERFORMANCE METRICS, AND INSTANCES OF TASKS WHICH REQUIRED DESIGN SKILLS TO EXECUTE.
ALIGNMENT	Is there a shared understanding of the organisation's vision between its front-line staff and executives? What could be done to achieve a better alignment? IT APPEARS THAT FRONT-LINE STAFF ARE NOT FAMILIAR WITH THE COMPANY'S VISION, BUT EXECUTIVES FEEL THAT THEY HAVE THIS COVERED. THIS SEEMS TO INDICATE THAT FRONT-LINE STAFF WEREN'T PART OF THE ORIGINAL VISION DEFINITION PROCESS AND THAT THE COMPANY'S VISION ISN'T WIDELY DISCUSSED (OR PART OF DECISION MAKING). TO IMPROVE ALIGNMENT THE COMPANY COULD RUN A SET OF WORKSHOPS (THAT INCLUDE FRONT-LINE STAFF) TO DEFINE A NEW VISION FOR THE ORGANISATION. THEY COULD ALSO LOOK FOR STORIES ABOUT FRONT-LINE STAFF THAT EMBODY THE COMPANIES VISION, AND DISSEMINATE THIS TO THE BROADER ORGANISATION.	Is there consensus about directive(s) between the organisation's front-line staff and executive? How could a concensus be reached? BOTH FRONT-LINE AND EXECUTIVE STAFF ARE AWARE OF DESIGN DIRECTIVES. HOWEVER, SEVERAL FRONT-LINE STAFF INDICATED THAT THEY WERE UNSURE OF WHY THESE DIRECTIVES EXISTED. THIS COULD INDICATE THAT WHILE THEY HAVE BEEN REQUESTED TO PRACTICE DESIGN, THEY ARE UNAWARE OF THE VALUE THAT IT COULD OFFER. INVOLVEMENT OF KEY STAFF IN DESIGN PROJECTS COULD DEMONSTRATE DESIGN'S VALUE, WHICH WOULD HELP THEM UNDERSTAND WHY THEY ARE BEING EXPECTED TO PRACTICE IT.

THE QUESTIONS IN LIGHT-GREY TEXT ARE JUST
STARTING POINTS! YOU'LL HAVE TO
ELABORATE AND PROBE WHEN TALKING TO
PEOPLE TO FIND THE INFORMATION YOU NEED.

FACILITIES

What spaces and resources do front-line staff believe are available to assist them in conducting their roles?

"I FEEL LIKE I ALWAYS GET THE SUPPORT I NEED TO COMPLETE A PROJECT, BUT FROM A HOLISTIC PERSPECTIVE I'M NOT REALLY SURE WHAT IS AVAILABLE TO ME".

AS THE ABOVE QUOTE, STAFF FELT VERY SUPPORTED - BUT WERE UNABLE TO MENTION ANY SPECIFIC FACILITIES AVAILABLE TO THEM.

What spaces and resources do executives believe have been provided to staff to assist them in conducting their roles and design?

"WE HAVE A STATE-OF-THE-ART PROJECT ROOM THAT CAN BE BOOKED OUT BY STAFF THAT NEED A SPACE THAT IS APPROPRIATE FOR DESIGN".

"A WHILE A GO WE SIGNED UP FOR A FEW SUBSCRIPTIONS TO SOFTWARE SUITES LIKE ADOBE CREATIVE CLOUD, WHICH WE ENCOURAGE OUR EMPLOYEES TO USE".

Are the available facilities and resources well known, understood and accessabile from both parties' perspectives? How could these facilities and resources become better known and accessed?

FRONT-LINE STAFF FEEL SUPPORTED, WHICH IS GOOD. NEVERTHELESS, THEY'RE NOT PARTICULARLY FAMILIAR WITH THE SUPPORT THAT IS AVAILABLE TO THEM. THE SOFTWARE SUITES IN PARTICULAR, WHICH HAVE A HIGH SUBSCRIPTION COST, SEEM TO BE UNDERUTILISED AND UNKNOWN.

BETTER METHODS FOR DISSEMINATING KNOWLEDGE ABOUT FACILITIES AVAILABLE FOR DESIGN SHOULD BE IMPLEMENTED.

CULTURAL CAPITAL

Do front-line staff believe they are supported (e.g. recieve sufficient training and support) to perform non-role specific directives (such as practicing design)? Are they aware of design's value?

"MANAGEMENT KEEPS SPROOKING HOW IMPORTANT DESIGN IS, BUT NOT REALLY SURE HOW THAT APPLIES TO ME".

"I WENT TO SOME DESIGN WORKSHOPS LAST YEAR WHICH I REALLY ENJOYED, BUT WAS NEVER REALLY SURE HOW TO IMPLEMENT WHAT I LEARNED INTO MY 'ACTUAL' JOB".

What efforts have been taken by the executive team to communicate the value of key initiatives (such as design practice) and to ensure that staff acquire the requisite skills to follow directive(s)?

"WE TALK ABOUT DESIGN ALL THE TIME. OUR MONTHLY NEWSLETTER ALWAYS HAS A SEGMENT ON IT!".

"YEP, WE HAD SOME DESIGN WORKSHOPS IN THE PAST WHICH OUR STAFF ABSOLUTELY LOVED".

Are perceptions of training and initiatives to support the organisation's core mandates aligned across front-line and executive staff? How could the need for such initiatives be identified, and the initiatives implemented?

BOTH FRONT-LINE AND EXECUTIVE STAFF ARE ON THE SAME PAGE IN TERMS OF THE TRAINING THAT HAS BEEN OFFERED. THE INQUIRY INTO 'DIRECTIVE(S)' REVEALED THAT SOME STAFF ARE NOT CONFIDENT IN THEIR DESIGN SKILLS.

IT ALSO APPEARS THAT STAFF ARE NOT AWARE OF WHY OR HOW DESIGN IS APPLICABLE TO THEM. THESE FACTORS INDICATE THAT TRAINING MIGHT HAVE FOCUSED TOO MUCH ON WHAT DESIGN IS RATHER THAN HOW AND WHY TO USE IT. THIS HIGHLIGHTS AN OPPORTUNITY TO REVISIT DESIGN TRAINING, AND TO BETTER ENGAGE FRONT-LINE STAFF IN PLANNING THIS TRAINING (PERHAPS BY GETTING THEM TO IDENTIFY AREAS NEEDING DEVELOPMENT).

GO TALK TO PEOPLE TO GET INFORMATION ABOUT THESE AREAS! IT DOESN'T NEED TO BE THROUGH FORMAL INTERVIEWS, IT COULD JUST BE A QUICK CHAT OVER LUNCH OR WHILE GOING ON A COFFEE RUN!.

THE ORGANISATIONAL CONDITIONS ARE NOT COMPLETELY RIGIT. SOMETIMES YOUR INQUIRY INTO A DIFFERENT CONDITION (IN THIS INSTANCE DIRECTIVES) CAN HELP WITH ANOTHER CONDITION.

THE STORY TOLD THROUGH THE ALIGNMENT CELLS IS PRETTY CLEAR. THE ORGANISATION HAS DONE A GREAT JOB INVESTING IN DESIGN AND EMBEDDING IT AS PART OF ITS AGENDA. HOWEVER, THE INTERNAL COMMNICATION AROUND THIS HAS BEEN A BIT LACKLUSTRE. IN THIS INSTANCE, THE ORGANISATIONAL CONDITIONS AUDIT HAS HIGHLIGHTED SOME PRETTY TANGIBLE STEPS THE ORGANISATION COULD TAKE - IT MIGHT NOT ALWAYS BE THIS CLEAR-CUT!

USE YOUR FINDINGS FROM THE ORIGINAL TOOL (PG. 58) OR FROM THE CONDITIONS AUDIT TO FILL IN THE CURRENT STATE (CELLS 1, 3, 5 & 7) AND INFORM THE OTHERS. WE'VE USED THE EXAMPLE ON THE PREVIOUS PAGE AS BACKGROUND INFORMATION FOR THIS MATRIX.

STRATEGIC VISION

1. STRATEGIC VISION

THE ORGANISATION HAS A VISION FOR THE FUTURE, BUT IT DOES NOT SEEM TO BE WELL DISSEMINATED WITH STAFF. IT WAS ALSO ESTABLISHED SEVERAL YEARS AGO AND NOT REVISITED, SO IT IS UNCLEAR IF IT ACCURATELY REFLECTS THE NEEDS OF CUSTOMERS.

Why is the organisation's vision what it is? How can this vision better align to stakeholder needs?

THE ORGANISATION'S VISION WAS FOUNDED ON INSIGHTS THAT THE CEO GAINED WHILE WORKING IN THE FIELD ON A PREVIOUS JOB. THESE INSIGHTS LED TO THE SUCCESS OF THE COMPANY - BUT HAVE NEVER BEEN REVISTED OR CHALLENGED. NEED TO TALK TO CUSOMERS TO SEE THE VISION STILL REFLECTS THEIR NEEDS.

2

3. DIRECTIVE(S)

STAFF ARE AWARE OF DESIGN DIRECTIVE(S), AND THESE ARE MEASURED FORMALLY AND INFORMALLY. THE RATIONALE BEHIND THE DIRECTIVES IS NOT WELL UNDERSTOOD.

How can the organisation leverage its directives to exemplify its vision?

THIS WOULD NOT BE ADVISED GIVEN THE POOR UNDERSTANDING BEHIND THE RATIONALE OF CURRENT DIRECTIVES. RECOMMENDED TO USE THE ORGANISATION'S VISION TO HELP REINFORCE THE DIRECTIVES INSTEAD.

ORGANISATIONS HAVE LIMITED CAPACITY. YOU NEED TO BE STRATEGIC WITH WHAT TO PRIORITISE.

5. FACILITIES

THE ORGANISATION HAS INVESTED IN RESOURCES FOR DESIGN, BUT STAFF ARE NOT WELL-ACQUAINTED WITH WHAT THESE ARE OR HOW THEY CAN BE ACCESSED. THERE ARE SOME NON-PERMANENT SPACES FOR DESIGN, BUT NO LONG-TERM ESTABLISHED HUB OR CENTRE. THIS INDICATED THE ORGANISATION FAVOURS SHORT PROJECTS RATHER THAN LONGER ENGAGEMENTS.

How can the organisation's spaces and resources reinforce its vision?

THE ORGANISATION'S VISION IS CURRENTLY COMMUNICATED THROUGH ITS WEBSITE, WHICH ISN'T BROWSED OFTEN BY STAFF (AS THERE IS NO REAL NEED TO). REINFORCING THE ORGANISATION'S VISION THROUGH PUBLIC OFFICE SPACES (SUCH AS THROUGH A POSTER OR GUIDE) COULD HELP DISSEMINATE THE VISION BETTER.

7. CULTURAL CAPITAL

STAFF HAVE RECIEVED SOME DESIGN TRAINING IN THE PAST. THERE IS A LACK IN CONFIDENCE AROUND HOW DESIGN CAN BE PRACTICED, AND THE VALUE OF DESIGN IS NOT WELL UNDERSTOOD.

How can the organisation's cultural capital help to frame its vision?

THEY JUST NEED TO BE CONSULTED IN THE CREATION OF THE VISION. THIS IS EVIDENT AS THEY ARE NOT FAMILIAR WITH WHAT IT IS.

DIRECTIVE(S)	FACILITIES	CULTURAL CAPITAL

How can the organisation's vision be used to inform the directive(s) given to staff?

THESE DO NOT SEEM TO BE LINKED AT PRESENT. THE ORGANISATION'S VISION COULD BE USED TO DEFINE AREAS OF STRATEGIC INTEREST, AND CORRESPONDING DIRECTIVES COULD HELP MEET OBJECTIVES IN THESE AREAS.

How can the organisation's vision be reflected in the spaces and resources it provides?

THE ORGANISATION HAS AN ESTABLISHED VISION (THAT IS NOT WIDELY UNDERSTOOD). WHILE THERE ARE RESOURCES FOR DESIGN, SPACES ARE LIMITED. A SEMI-PERMANENT BASE OR HUB FOR DESIGN COULD HELP REINFORCE THE ORGANISATION'S VISION AND ESTABLISH THAT ITS SERIOUS ABOUT DESIGN.

How can the organisation's vision be communicated to its people?

DESIGN TRAINING THAT FOCUSES ON SHARING INSIGHTS FROM THE ORGANISATION'S DESIGN INITIATIVES COULD HELP TO REINFORCE THE ORGANISATIONS VISION. REGULAR COMMUNICATIONS (E.G. THROUGH A WEEKLY NEWSLETTER) COULD ALSO HELP REINFORCE THIS.

What is the rationale behind the organisation's current directive(s)? Are there mechanisms ensuring these directive(s) are followed?

THE CEO, AND SOME EXECUTIVES, HAVE SEEN THE VALUE AND BENEFITS OF DESIGN (HENCE THE DIRECTIVES FOR IT). USE OF DESIGN IS MEASURED THROUGH KPIS, BUT STAFF DON'T REALLY UNDERSTAND WHY THEY REQUIRE DESIGN.

How can the organisation leverage its directive(s) to improve its environment?

BASED ON THE CURRENT STATE THERE IS NO CLEAR LINK BETWEEN THESE CONDITIONS, BEST TO IDENTIFY OPPORTUNITIES ELSEWHERE.

How can the organisation's directive(s) be used to shape its cultural capital?

THE ORGANISATION'S PEOPLE KNOW WHAT THEY ARE REQUIRED TO DO, BUT NOT NECESSARILY WHY. THIS KNOWLEDGE COULD BE MORE EXPLICITLY BUILT INTO INDUCTION AND TRAINING.

4

How can the organisation better equip its people (through resources and spaces) to follow the directive(s) given?

THE MAJOR ISSUE SEEMS TO BE A LACK OF AWARENESS OF WHAT RESOURCES AND SPACES ARE AVAILABLE FOR STAFF. BETTER COMMUNICATION OF WHAT THESE ARE AND HOW THEY CAN BE ACCESSED WOULD HELP STAFF FOLLOW THE DIRECTIVES.

Why are the organisation's facilities the way they are? How can they be improved?

THEY HAVE ARISEN ORGANICALLY. SOME RESOURCES HAVE BEEN ACQUIRED BASED ON THE EXECUTIVE TEAM'S ASSUMPTIONS. TALKING WITH EMPLOYEES ABOUT BARRIERS TO DOING THEIR JOBS, AND WHAT ELSE THEY REQUIRE TO BE EFFECTIVE COULD HELP HIGHLIGHT ROOM FOR IMPROVEMENT.

How can the organisation's facilities best serve its people?

STRONG CORRELATION HERE WITH THE FACILITIES X DIRECTIVES CELL. MORE AWARENESS OF THE AVAILABLE SPACES AND RESOURCES WOULD BE OF MONUMENTAL HELP.

DON'T BE AFRAID OF REPETITION! SOMETIMES REINFORCING THE SAME POINT CAN HELP ESTABLISH WHAT IS IMPORTANT.

6

How can the organisation's people be supported to follow the directive(s) given?

ADDITIONAL OVERSIGHT OVER WHY THE PARTICULAR DIRECTIVES THEY HAVE WERE GIVEN WOULD HELP THEM UNDERSTAND WHY THEY SHOULD BE FOLLOWING THEM. ADDITIONAL TRAINING (SUCH AS A WORKSHOP) WHICH BETTER ARTICULATES THE VALUE OF THE DIRECTIVES WOULD ALSO BE BENEFICIAL.

How can the organisation's cultural capital inform the design of its spaces and the acquisition of resources?

NO CLEAR LINK IN THIS INSTANCE.

NOT EVERY CELL NEEDS TO BE FILLED IN. SOMETIMES YOU WON'T FIND A CLEAR RELATIONSHIP IN THE DATA, AND ITS FINE TO ADMIT THAT. DON'T FORCE SOMETHING THAT ISN'T THERE.

Why is the organisation's cultural capital in its current state and composition? Does it reflect the organisation's needs?

THERE DOESN'T SEEM TO BE ANY STRATEGIC REASON FOR THE ORGANISATION'S CURRENT STATE FOR CULTURAL CAPITAL. THE ORGANISATION IS DOING WELL, SO THEY LIKELY HAVE THE SKILLS THEY REQUIRE. DESIGN SEEMS TO BE A PRIORITY FOR EXECUTIVES, BUT NOT FOR FRONT-LINE STAFF.

8

THINKING STYLES

THINKING STYLES

Innovation requires many different perspectives, ideas and approaches. These are representative of diverse groups of people and have origins in a spectrum of disciplines. We all view the world differently, and this needs to be taken into account when practicing design. Here we describe how design fits within the broader cognitive biases of most firms. We present three thinking styles (systems thinking, design thinking, and creative thinking) to demonstrate how people solve problems. It is proposed that design thinking balances systems thinking and creative thinking by building a bridge between the aims, methods, and results of the other two approaches.

The seminal authority on thinking styles, De Bono (1989), established that the conscious use of different types of thinking for distinct objectives can lead to an increase in competence. He also explains that different styles of thinking can form 'thought-roles' that can be employed as required in a project. Thinking styles are described as the different ways of governing or managing activities in a preferred style to represent and process information (Thompson et al., 2012). It is how individuals prefer to use the cognitive abilities they possess, rather 'what' they are thinking about (Sternberg, 1999). Thinking styles can contribute to innovation and, in some cases, differing thinking styles can help produce a positive organisational culture. Researchers have noted that there is a substantial relationship between thinking styles and risk taking, creativity and innovation (Dean et al., 2008; Ghobadi & Shoghi, 2013).

In recent decades, the pursuit of understanding thinking styles has gained much attention in organisational behaviour and management literature (Broeck, Vanderheyden & Cools, 2003). Thinking styles often differ and include varying approaches to:

✕ PERCEIVING AND ASSIMILATING DATA.
✕ MAKING DECISIONS
✕ SOLVING PROBLEMS
✕ RELATING TO OTHER PEOPLE.

Conflicting thinking styles in a team can result in tension. Naturally, an understanding of others' preferences in thinking style can help facilitate communication, collaboration, and innovation (Leonard & Straus, 1997). An organisation's management must understand that people have different thinking styles. Managers who dislike conflict or only value their own approach (or the organisation's preferred approach) often actively avoid the clash of ideas and styles. This phenomenon is referred to as 'comfortable clone syndrome', where co-workers share similar interests and training and think alike, therefore limiting the potential for innovation to occur (Thompson, Tongo, & Chhabriya, 2012). Leonard & Straus (1997) explain that a new-business development group formed entirely of employees with the same disciplinary background and set of experiences will struggle to innovate, as they will assess every idea with an unvarying set of assumptions and analytical tools.

We explore three approaches to innovation their corresponding thinking styles:
1. SYSTEMS
2. DESIGN
3. CREATIVE.

SYSTEMS THINKING

Systems Thinking, of the three cognitive thinking styles explored here, represents the simplest thinking style for exploration. Unlike Design Thinking or Creative Thinking, Systems Thinking involves a clearly defined, tangible process with proven and predictable outcomes and specific characteristics. Systems Thinking was developed out of the School of Management at MIT. Its history stretches back to the 1950s and is intertwined with business and industry (Jackson, 2009). Since its inception, the thinking style has since permeated the fields of psychology, biology, and sociology. It has been a staple in organisational management science and health circles due to its clear definition, process, technique and simple educational methods.

The style can be defined as an analytical approach in which multiple steps or parts are arranged and rearranged to arrive at a suitable solution. Senge (2006) defines Systems Thinking as a framework for seeing interrelationships rather than things; a process to see patterns and changing dynamics. Senge's definition relates to holistically seeing a process, understanding that individual elements exist within a context and that there are interrelationships between those elements. By viewing a problem, system or organisation in this way, it is possible to achieve vastly different results, ideas or techniques than if one analysed individual pieces of data in isolation.

DESIGN THINKING

Design Thinking (which is discussed at length at the start of the book) is explained by Brown (2008, 2009) as an intangible, unquantifiable way of thinking. It enables a person to rapidly prototype and assess concepts and arrive at optimal answers or solutions. The thinking style uses the skills designers possess to create advantageous solutions to a vast range of problems. This is accomplished by emphasising human-centeredness and creating value for stakeholders. There are many schools of thought for Design Thinking, resulting in a number of different approaches for the thinking style. The basis of Design Thinking is the skills possessed by designers. However, the style evolved into a clearly quantified set of attributes that design thinkers possess, and finally to articulated frameworks for funnelling knowledge and practically applying design skills to solve problems (Holloway, 2009).

CREATIVE THINKING

Creativity, and thus the process of Creative Thinking, has been highly debated in various fields (primarily cognitive psychology) for decades. Seminal work includes Wallas's (1926) book The Art of Thought and Osborn's (1953) Applied Imagination. These texts have influenced the theories of creative thinking. Mednick (1962, 221) defines the Creative Thinking process as the 'forming of associative elements into new combinations which either meet specified requirements or are in some way useful'. Hayes (1989) defines a creative act by three characteristics associated with the output. It must:

THE GUY WHO COINED BRAINSTORMING!

X BE ORIGINAL OR NOVEL
X BE SEEN AS VALUABLE OR INTERESTING
X REFLECT WELL ON THE MIND OF THE CREATOR.

According to Almeida et. al (2008), Creative Thinking has five loose characteristics. It:

1. is more commonly associated with divergent thinking than convergent thinking
2. is more an individual attribute than a universal one
3. revolves around insight and novelty rather than a learning routine or behaviour
4. is commonly associated with problem finding as opposed to problem solving
5. is about the association (even if loosely related) when generating ideas as opposed to spontaneous or frequent ideas.

There are many techniques and frameworks for discovering and harnessing Creative Thinking, and thus there are many approaches to teaching it (Michalko, 2010). Notably, Creative Thinking is (paradoxically) hindered by and excels due to a lack of definition and strict procedure. This flexibility allows for solutions that are radically different from those emerging from thinking styles that follow a strict procedure.

KARLA'S DESK
"EMPTY DESK, EMPTY MIND?"

UNDERSTANDING THE DIFFERENT THINKING STYLES

The following example has been used to illustrate how the three thinking styles can result in different outcomes when responding to the same design brief. We have also included an activity (THINKING STYLES) that illustrates how the thinking styles result in different ideas (this is a great chance for you to write on this book if you have not done so already). For this example, we are going to look at 'innovating the tourist experience of the Eiffel Tower'. This activity could be run this with any project or design brief. Each of the thinking styles is then explained through three simple steps. You can follow these steps for your own project or brief using the template at the back of the book.

SYSTEMS THINKING APPROACH

1. The first step is to breakdown the current experience for a tourist visiting the Eiffel Tower into simple phases. You could expand the experience to start even further back in time, for example, seeing an advertisement about the Eiffel Tower, planning the trip, etc. In this instance we are framing the start of the experience as arrival at the Eiffel Tower, with the categorisation of these phases:

COME - WAIT - PAY - WAIT - ENJOY - LEAVE

2. The next step is to work out the desired focus of the intended solutions, such as making it cheaper, faster, customer-oriented, reducing complaints, safer, fun, or to maximise profit.

3. The final step is to investigate the options detailed in step 2 through different 'patterns' to re-design the current phases in the tourist experience. Examples of patterns include eliminating, improving, re-sequencing and specialising one or all of the steps.

FOR EXAMPLE, you could re-sequence the order of payment and queue, so that payment is made upon departure. This would reduce the waiting time and provide a more attractive offer, resulting in more paying customers.

DESIGN THINKING APPROACH

1. Start with understanding the customer and their problem(s) in relation to the experience. A fundamental step includes asking the question, 'what is the problem through the customer's eyes?' You could use a range of tools discussed throughout this book to explore this question.

2. The next step is to conceptualise possible solutions to the customer problem. For example, by asking 'what are some possible solutions to solve that problem, but more importantly what is the real meaning behind the solution?'

3. The final step is to explore these ideas through the use of a narrative[9] focused on the customer experience, with a specific focus on the 'pains' and 'gains' of the experience. During this step you also need to question 'what is the value proposition of the organisation?' The aim of this approach is to produce radical innovation by understanding the customer experience and aligning it with the company's strategic direction.

AN EXAMPLE of an idea could be providing French photo props (moustache, wheel of cheese, berets, wine bottle) which are rented out for a small price while on top of the Eiffel Tower. The Tourist then take photos on their own phones, which they can then opt to be projected from the Eiffel Tower onto the ground below for a few seconds, sharing their experience with everyone.

IT IS IMPORTANT TO FOCUS ON QUANTITY, NOT QUALITY. ENSURE NO IDEA IS OVERLOOKED.

CREATIVE THINKING APPROACH[10]

1. Start with imagining the experience. Think about what it could be and what it might not be. Then, draw all your ideas on what the experience could be or should not be.

2. Repeat the first step again with this new experience in mind.

3. Now take two unlikely ideas – things that wouldn't necessarily go together – and try to create a mash-up of them; explore the best way these ideas could be integrated. The aim of this approach is to take things to the unexpected, so you might need to go back to step 1 and 2 to think of more unusual ideas. Remember that no idea is "TOO CRAZY", farfetched or not possible.

AN EXAMPLE outcome might be applying the experience of a blind date and extreme sports. Two people could meet on top of the Eiffel Tower and, if they like each other, opt to parachute off the Eiffel Tower together (as we said, no idea is too crazy!).
THOUGH THIS ONE IS PROBABLY BAD. MAYBE?

---

[9] A design narrative can be used as a discussion tool in qualitative research to convey a story and its characters in relation to a specific problem or opportunity, or to test a design output or concept. The narrative can help test the designer's assumptions surrounding the design context, or to understand stakeholders perspectives on a problem, opportunity or design.

[10] Even though there is no defined approach for Creative Thinking, we have provided three steps for you to follow.

INTEGRATED THINKING

In today's business environment it is critical for organisations to innovate. However, innovating is not a simple task. Many firms struggle to innovate due to conflicting thinking styles (which make collaboration difficult) (Armstrong, Cools & Sadler; Smith, 2012). While many factors can aid or hinder an organisation's ability to innovate, facilitating collaboration among individuals who view problems in inherently different ways can be of significant value.

Organisations need to innovate not only during the conception stage but throughout the development and implementation stages of design. It is also important to understand the type of innovation a project requires before starting it, as this can help inform what people should be involved. The distinction between refining an existing design or system (incremental innovation) and introducing a new concept (radical or disruptive innovation) is important in considering thinking styles and the coordination of multi-disciplinary teams. Incremental innovation only reinforces an organisation's existing capabilities, whereas radical innovation forces the organisation to explore new, uncertain futures and to adopt different skillsets and approaches. Incremental and radical innovation requires different organisational approaches and individual capabilities. These need to be grounded in complementary thinking styles, which can be difficult for managers to prioritise beyond their own personal approach (Henderson & Clark, 1990).

You will probably know what thinking style you typically use (or used in the last activity) and hopefully have a sound understanding of your own cognitive processes. Each of these can be broadly associated with either the 'right' or 'left' brain. If we take the solution of the systems thinker, we could categorise it into a typical 'left-brain' approach, which consists of linear and analytical thinking. Conversely, a creative approach is usually associated with 'right-brain' tendencies and is described as a more sensory, creative, and emotional response to a task. A design thinker may not conform to either the left or right brain definitions. They can be expected to adopt aspects from both.

To provide a structured process, we have created a simple model to follow when undertaking a project. The model (INTEGRATED THINKING) outlines a recommended process for combining the strengths of each thinking style into one approach. This model could be used to help different thinking styles work together or just to understand the strengths and weakness of each approach. The process begins with understanding the current system and breaking it down into steps (SYSTEM THINKING); ideas are then generated using the Creative Thinking approach of imagining what could be, placing ideas together, and then taking things to the extreme. These ideas are then developed through a Design Thinking approach which ensures the ideas are desirable, feasible, and viable (and that the identified issue has been addressed). This would be done by testing the idea by describing the solution in a narrative form and making it concrete through aligning it with the organisation's value proposition. Throughout the process, ideas are moving between the abstract and concrete, through the phases of conception, development and implementation – so as to not limit the formation of radical ideas.

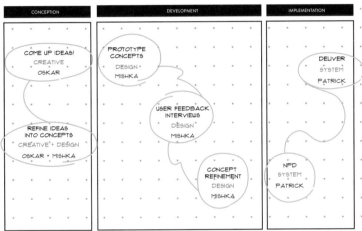

1: WRITE THE MAIN TASKS TO COMPLETE ACROSS THE THREE STAGES

2: WRITE WHAT THINKING STYLE WOULD BE BEST SUITED TO COMPLETE THE TASK

3: FOR EACH TASK WRITE THE NAME OF SOMEONE IN YOUR PROJECT TEAM WHO IS BEST SUITED FOR THE TASK.

4: DRAW A LINE TO CONNECT ALL THE TASK PERFORMED BY THE SAME PERSON.

Thinking styles can have a major impact and influence on project outcomes and are thus important for organisation's seeking to integrate design. We hope that the (THINKING STYLES) activity and the simple process outlined have helped to introduce the three different styles; and assisted you to form a better understanding of and appreciation for the different approaches. Remember that each thinking style offers an inherently different set of tools and approaches, all of which have value. Understanding the logic and value of the different styles can also assist you to break down barriers to collaboration when working with individuals with different backgrounds. The aim of including different thinking styles is to allow organisations to better utilise and leverage the benefits of multi-disciplinary teams with varying thinking styles.

TAKEAWAYS

X DIFFERENT THINKING STYLES AFFECT THE OUTCOME AND DEVELOPMENT OF A SOLUTION.

X THROUGH AWARENESS, COMPARISON, AND ANALYSIS OF DIFFERENT STYLES YOU WILL GAIN A BETTER UNDERSTANDING OF THEM AND HOW THEY CAN BE MANAGED AND LEVERAGED OFF ONE ANOTHER.

X EACH THINKING STYLE OFFERS INHERENTLY DIFFERENT TANGIBLE TOOLS AND APPROACHES, ALL OF WHICH HAVE VALUE.

X ORGANISATIONS CAN BREAK DOWN BARRIERS TO COLLABORATION BY UNDERSTANDING THE VALUE OF THE DIFFERENT THINKING STYLES.

X ORGANISATIONS NEED TO GET BETTER AT UTILISING AND LEVERAGING THE BENEFITS OF MULTI-DISCIPLINARY TEAMS WITH VARYING THINKING STYLES.

DESIGN PRINCIPLES

(THEORETICALLY)
F.A.Q

DESIGN PRINCIPLES

As designers, this is our chance to offer some unsolicited advice. Our work with a plethora of organisations has helped us to synthesise a set of principles to guide practitioners of design innovation. These include prescriptive statements on how to scope and implement design innovation, normative advice on what not to do as well as tips for achieving design integration. They are not a checklist per se, but a set of guidelines to keep in mind as you practice design. Some of them might seem obvious, but in an emerging field clarity never hurts. The original set of principles can be used by a design catalyst but should also be embraced organisation-wide. We have synthesised the principles into a list of problems that you may face as a design practitioner and offer a brief guide for how these might be tackled.

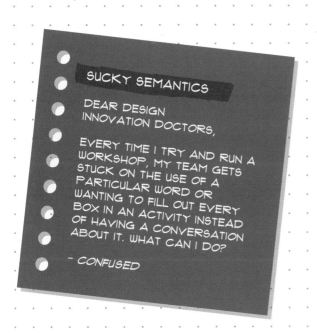

SUCKY SEMANTICS

DEAR DESIGN INNOVATION DOCTORS,

EVERY TIME I TRY AND RUN A WORKSHOP, MY TEAM GETS STUCK ON THE USE OF A PARTICULAR WORD OR WANTING TO FILL OUT EVERY BOX IN AN ACTIVITY INSTEAD OF HAVING A CONVERSATION ABOUT IT. WHAT CAN I DO?

- CONFUSED

NO CULTURE

DEAR DESIGN INNOVATION DOCTORS,

I AM STRUGGLING TO CHANGE THE CULTURE REQUIRED TO EMBRACE DESIGN INNOVATION. WHAT CAN I DO TO HELP THIS?

-STRUGGLING

Visualisation methods allow for those in different roles and professions, who use different terminology, to share ideas and brainstorm without being hindered by strict definitions. Visual thinking leads to less time talking (more commonly arguing) and more time doing (collaborating and solving the problem). This is where many of the tools in our book can assist. Tools are not the answer, but they do help facilitate the conversation – allowing the right questions to be asked. Design innovation consists of more than just a toolset. It is the combination of tools, thinking styles, and processes. The value of tools expands beyond their intended use to include facilitation of communication, permission to think creatively, and learning and teaching through visualisation (Straker & Wrigley, 2014). Remember – design tools facilitate the process, not the solution.

DR S's TOP TIP: STAY CLEAR OF BUZZWORDS, STICK TO TERMS THAT ARE WELL-KNOWN AND USED IN THE ORGANISATION.

DR W's TOP TIP: THE DESIGN TOOL IS IRRELEVANT IF YOU DO NOT KNOW WHAT YOU ARE TRYING TO ACHIEVE WITH IT.

Design Innovation can assist (is not a substitute for) cultural change or transformational programs within organisations. These transformations can require a shift in several critical aspects of what defines the business:

✗ its culture
✗ its organisational structure
✗ the way the business interacts

with or engages with its customers.
Such transformations are rarely successful without collaboration across all organisational departments and functions. Early buy-in is required in order for the organisation as a whole to own and accept the change. Design innovation applies a process of understanding a problem coupled with possible solutions to make this happen.

DR S's TOP TIP: START SMALL. START WITH A SMALLER PROJECT, WITH A FEW KEY PEOPLE. THIS WAY IT IS LESS RISKY AND YOU WILL BE ABLE TO DEMONSTRATE THE VALUE OF THE PROCESS.

DR N's TOP TIP: THE PROOF IS IN THE PUDDING. IF YOU'RE HAVING TROUBLE GETTING PEOPLE TO EMBRACE DESIGN THEN YOU NEED TO DEMONSTRATE ITS VALUE (E.G., THROUGH A LOW-RISK DESIGN PROJECT).

DR W's TOP TIP: IF YOU CAN FIND ONE GOOD PERSON WILLING TO JOIN A COALITION OF THE WILLING THIS IS A GREAT START!

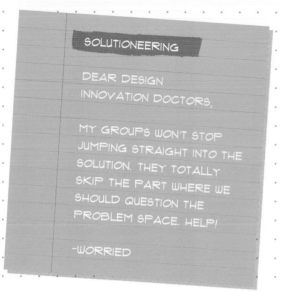

SOLUTIONEERING

DEAR DESIGN
INNOVATION DOCTORS,

MY GROUPS WON'T STOP
JUMPING STRAIGHT INTO THE
SOLUTION. THEY TOTALLY
SKIP THE PART WHERE WE
SHOULD QUESTION THE
PROBLEM SPACE. HELP!

-WORRIED

Frequently, jumping to a solution without fully understanding the problem causes shallow band-aid solutions that don't actually address the problem. More is to be gained by uncovering a customer's real issues, needs, and desires than by being first to market with an undesired product. Understanding these aspects places a company in a better position to produce desired products or services, providing them a competitive advantage. This can be seen when teams are sent out to customers' homes to listen to their problems instead of selling them the firm's services. The new skill of listening to the problems of customers, questioning if their service did indeed offer value, and if it solved any unresolved customer issues (Stevenson, Wrigley & Matthews, 2015) is always eye opening.

DR S's TOP TIP: LET THEM GET ALL THEIR IDEAS OUT, SPEND TIME ALLOWING EVERYONE TO SHARE AND DISCUSS ANY IDEAS. ONCE THIS IS DONE YOU CAN ASK THAT THEY CONTINUE TO WRITE DOWN IDEAS BUT PROVIDE CLEAR PRIORITIES THROUGHOUT THE PROJECT TO KEEP THEM ON TRACK.

DR W's TOP TIP: SLOW IS STEADY - STEADY IS FAST.

FEELING ISOLATED

DEAR DESIGN
INNOVATION DOCTORS,

MY ORGANISATION IS VERY
TRADITIONAL WITH EACH
DEPARTMENT WORKING IN
ISOLATION. DO YOU THINK I
SHOULD TRY TO GET THEM TO
ENGAGE MORE?

- CONCERNED

Design can bridge many disciplines and help to de-silo innovation efforts. For change to gather momentum there needs to be an understanding of all operational levels of the organisation and the needs of internal and external stakeholders. This cannot happen where innovation is considered the realm of responsibility of one department or corporate function. Design innovation engages those previously not involved in the innovation pipeline to table their ideas and provide alternate perspectives not previously considered.

DR W's TOP TIP: YOU KNOW WHAT THEY SAY - IT IS BETTER TO HAVE THESE PEOPLE INSIDE THE TENT PISSING OUT THAN OUTSIDE PISSING IN!

DR N's TOP TIP: TRY TO ORGANISE SOME FUN, VOLUNTARY DESIGN ACTIVITIES (SUPPORTED BY YOUR DESIGN CHAMPION) THAT SHARE KEY INSIGHTS FROM YOUR WORK. THIS SHOULD HELP INCREASE INTEREST IN COLLABORATION!

DR S's TOP TIP: FINISH EVERY FRIDAY AT 4PM AND GO TO THE PUB, MEETING OUTSIDE THE OFFICE MIGHT HELP PEOPLE 'DE-SILO'.

Design teaches the value of the customer perspective. By focusing on the customer, and asking and answering every question from their perspective, it makes sure they are at the centre of everything the organisation does and everything they stand for. Customers and markets change rapidly and disconnecting from them can be a common problem for many organisations. Design innovation can assist with uncovering latent customer needs for the customers you already have (in captivity) and those who are yet to be your customers (in the wild). Design Innovation methods are able to provide fresh, non-obvious ways of understanding customer needs, problems and behaviours that can become the foundation of new business opportunities (Price, Wrigley & Straker, 2015). They provide a critical layer to understand why customers do and don't engage with businesses. Design innovation allows these needs to be leveraged into new products or services, and perhaps ultimately a changed business model.

DR W's TOP TIP: IT'S MORE LIKE WORK-LIFE INTEGRATION (NOT BALANCE). IF YOU ARE NOT DREAMING ABOUT HOW TO IMPROVE THINGS YOU ARE NOT WORKING HARD ENOUGH!

DR S's TOP TIP: CUSTOMER ENGAGEMENT DOES NOT NEED TO BE AT A LARGE SCALE. A COUPLE OF IN-DEPTH CONVERSATIONS WITH CUSTOMERS COULD GET YOU BACK ON TRACK.

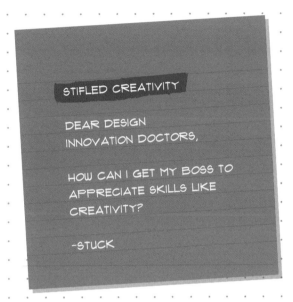

Creativity is not a skill rewarded by many organisations – design can provide a platform for radical thinking. Conservative growth targets chased by senior management are usually in response to corporate bonus structures, negating the drive for longer term, more radical innovations. Playing it safe can only lead to incremental changes. Radical changes may be required to generate value, however corporate culture can prevent individuals from coming forward with drastically different ideas. Design innovation promotes the sharing of disruptive ideas and provides an environment where such ideas are encouraged. Risk taking, originality, and anticipation of future trends are rewarded.

DR S's TOP TIP: IF IT DOESN'T WORK OUT AND YOU FIND YOURSELF SPENDING MOST OF YOUR TIME TRYING TO CONVINCE YOUR BOSS OF THE IMPORTANCE OF IT, MAYBE IT'S TIME TO FIND A NEW JOB.

DR W's TOP TIP: YOU CAN'T – PEOPLE DON'T LEAVE JOBS THEY LEAVE BOSSES!

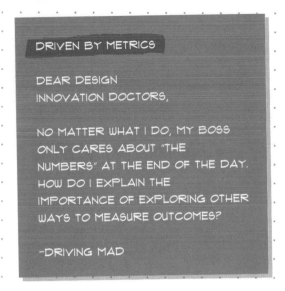

DRIVEN BY METRICS

DEAR DESIGN
INNOVATION DOCTORS,

NO MATTER WHAT I DO, MY BOSS
ONLY CARES ABOUT "THE
NUMBERS" AT THE END OF THE DAY.
HOW DO I EXPLAIN THE
IMPORTANCE OF EXPLORING OTHER
WAYS TO MEASURE OUTCOMES?

-DRIVING MAD

SCARED TO FAIL

DEAR DESIGN
INNOVATION DOCTORS,

I AM FINDING IT CHALLENGING
TO EMBRACE 'FAILURE'. WHAT
DO?

-AFRAID

Incentives drive behaviour. KPIs targeting incremental improvements form obstacles to real transformational change. Therefore, alternatives to traditional KPIs must be supported by upper management to change existing behaviours. Once the first project is delivered utilising a design innovation approach the outcomes (results) and these returns on investments can be measured and evaluated. The value of the design innovation process becomes clear, and in turn, an increased appetite for this approach to innovation can be disseminated in additional departments of the organisation. However, depending on the industry and product this can take time. So patients is a virtue.

DR W's TOP TIP: ALWAYS HAVE ANOTHER TRICK UP YOUR PONY DECK!

DR N's TOP TIP: GET GOOD AT READING AND FIDDLING WITH SPREADSHEETS!

Design crafts fast prototypes, as failure is often a necessary part of success. The concept of failing fast is intrinsically linked to the notion that all ideas are valid and worthy of further testing. As a minimum, failures should generate data on what doesn't work, and prompt a company to further investigate why. Failures can only be tolerable as part of a process that accepts them as such. Design-integrated companies with the correct mindset or attitude know this and benefit from it. They benefit from less buy-in resistance, sustained momentum towards a solution, and faster prototypes.

DR S's TOP TIP: AS LONG AS YOU ARE ACTIVELY LEARNING FROM EACH 'FAILURE' YOU ARE DOING IT RIGHT.

DR W's TOP TIP: LEARN TO PRACTICE WHAT YOU PREACH. MY FIRST MENTOR TOLD ME THIS - IF YOU DON'T STAND FOR SOMETHING YOU WILL FALL FOR ANYTHING.

(DIDN'T BATMAN SAY THAT? WAIT IS BATMAN YOUR MENTOR?)

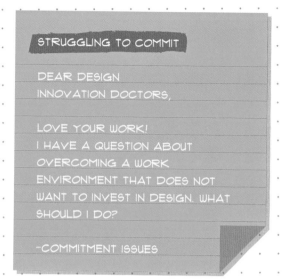

Design innovation is a process focused on business transformation. Nurturing and developing a culture of innovation within a business is a long-term process requiring a vision for the future shaped by market analysis and deep customer insights. It requires access to valuable company resources, which may include production capacity, key personnel and substantial funding. These requirements cannot be met in an environment where a reduction in costs is considered the key driver of long-term profitability or competitive advantage. Though design innovation is an iterative process with no scheduled endpoint, for its application to be successful, design innovation should be resourced with the same discipline and thoughtfulness as any large, complex, or important project. Similarly, roles within the design innovation team – such as the design catalyst – are full-time roles, requiring a commitment to the entire process.

DR N's TOP TIP: IDENTIFY AND WIN OVER THE KEY DECISION MAKERS, THEY CAN HELP YOU SET UP AN AGENDA FOR DESIGN.

DR W's TOP TIP: GET TO KNOW THE PEOPLE AT THE TOP AND HOW YOU PITCH DESIGNS WORTH TO THEM.

Sorry, we're not those kinds of doctors. As we mentioned in our recent book, design is not a silver bullet or the solution to every problem.

DR S's TOP TIP: PERHAPS OUR OTHER BOOK DESIGN INNOVATION FOR HEALTH AND MEDICINE WILL BE MORE USEFUL. (SHAMELESS PLUG)

DR W's TOP TIP: WHAT SHE SAID!

TAKEAWAYS

✗ THESE ARE NOT STRICT RULES TO FOLLOW.

✗ SOME OF THESE WILL APPLY TO YOU MORE THAN OTHERS AND CAN BE USED IN COMBINATION.

✗ TO BE USED ONLY AS SUGGESTIONS IF YOUR ORGANISATION IS HAVING SUCH PROBLEMS OR ISSUES.

✗ SITTING BEHIND EACH OF THESE PRINCIPLES OR GUIDELINE SUGGESTIONS ARE A PLETHORA OF TOOLS, TEMPLATES, AND METHODS THAT CAN BE USED TO HELP FACILITATE DESIGN PRACTICE (REMEMBER YOU ARE NOT ALONE ON THE JOURNEY)

CONCLUSION

Designers are increasingly rising to the upper echelons of business, with titles such as Chief Customer Officer and Chief Design Officer. Such leadership roles begin to cement design's value at the executive level. A seat at the boardroom table, yay! Businesses are not only becoming aware of the value of design, but learning how to harness it to tackle complex problems and meet the needs of stakeholders.

The path to design integration is not an easy one. It is rife with barriers. For instance, a managerial preoccupation with return on investment or staff absorbed in achieving their KPIs. These can make it difficult to embrace design, and to build a rich design capability and culture within an organisation. Transparency, trust and bold leaders are key to overcoming these challenges.

This book has introduced you to the concepts of design innovation and integration; detailed the components of the design innovation framework; and provided a glimpse of what you should expect when embarking on your own design adventure. We hope you have marked up the book with your thoughts and ideas – and that you are ready to leap off the pages and into practice. The templates provided at the back of this book are here to help scaffold your design journey. As we have stressed, the templates are by no means the blueprint for your success. They are just a starting point! Good luck!

IT'S YOUR TIME TO FLY!.

FLY HIGH!.

TOOL TEMPLATES

200   ORGANISATIONAL CONDITIONS FRAMEWORK
201   STAKEHOLDER MAP
202   BUSINESS MODEL CONTENT ANALYSIS
203   CUSTOMER SEGMENT PROFILES
204   MARKET DISRUPTORS
205   BUSINESS MODEL SWOT
206   PLOT THE COMPETITION
207   SEGMENTING CUSTOMERS
208   PRODUCT ANALYSIS
209   VALUE DEFINITION
210   DESIGN BRIEF
211   DEFINING YOUR PHILOSOPHY
212   VISUALISE YOUR PRACTICE
213   DESIGN CRITERIA
214   SOLUTION EVALUATION
215   DESIGNING INNOVATIVE PRODUCTS
216   CIRCLE CREATION
217   INNOVATION MASHING
218   MR SQUIGGLE
219   POST-IT NOTE PICTIONARY
220   LETTERS AND NUMBERS
221   PROTOTYPE PLAN
222   PITCHING
223   PRODUCT CLASSIFICATION MATRIX
224   3 HORIZONS
225   JOHNSON & JONES MATRIX
226   DESIGN CATALYST
227   DESIGN CATALYST CAPABILITIES
228   ORGANISATIONAL CONDITION AUDIT
229   ORGANISATIONAL CONDITION MATRIX
230   THINKING STYLES
231   INTEGRATED THINKING

ORGANISATIONAL CONDITIONS FRAMEWORK

DESIGN INNOVATION & INTEGRATION STRAKER, WRIGLEY & NUSEM 2020

GAINING INSIGHT ON THE ORGANISATION

The organisational conditions framework is structured to help the user to understand an organisation's strategic vision, directive(s), facilities and cultural capital. A set of questions is posed for each of the organisational conditions in order to help the user inquire about the respective states of the conditions within an organisation. These questions are merely starting points – they are not an exhaustive list of what should be considered. Anything relating to the conditions can be populated into the columns. **Work through each of the columns by following the guiding questions and noting anything else of relevance.**

STRATEGIC VISION

An organisation's overall vision and value proposition – describing the organisation's strategic direction, it's appetite for change or innovation, and its risk aversion.

- Does the organisation have a vision for the future (an aim or mission)?
- Does the organisation have appetite for change or innovation?

DIRECTIVE(S)

The organisation's directives which denote that the organisation's people are accountable in demonstrating and practicing design.

- Are the organisation's people held accountable in practicing design?
- Are there key performance indicators which detail design practice?
- Are there roles in the organisation which reflect design practice?

FACILITIES

The organisation's facilities, referring to the extent to which it supports emerging design initiatives (with a focus on the physical environment and resources):

- Is design given a space within the organisation?
- Are the required resources for design provided?

CULTURAL CAPITAL

The capacity of the organisation's people in practicing design – i.e. their knowledge of how to practice design and their understanding of the value it offers.

- Do the organisation's people know how to practice design?
- Do the organisation's people understand the value design offers?

200

STAKEHOLDER MAP

OUTLINING KEY PLAYERS

DESIGN INNOVATION & INTEGRATION STRAKER, WRIGLEY & NUSEM, 2020

We present two templates for mapping stakeholders: concentric circles and the power versus interest grid. The concentric circles model is perhaps the simplest one.

STEP 1: Create a comprehensive list of stakeholders.

STEP 2: Determine the value for your three layers. This could be [core / direct / indirect], [essential / important / interesting] or something else entirely. For clarity, circle the set you have selected or write your own values over the labels.

STEP 3: Plot each stakeholder according to which group it fits into.

The power versus interest grid offers a way to classify an organisation's stakeholders according to their power and interest. It will help you to identify which stakeholders must be taken into account (either to arrive at an optimal solution, without which the project cannot succeed, that are required to fully understand the problem, etc.).

STEP 1: Create a comprehensive list of stakeholders.

STEP 2: Plot each of the stakeholders according to their interest and power (note: you could create your own axes and new labels for each quadrant).

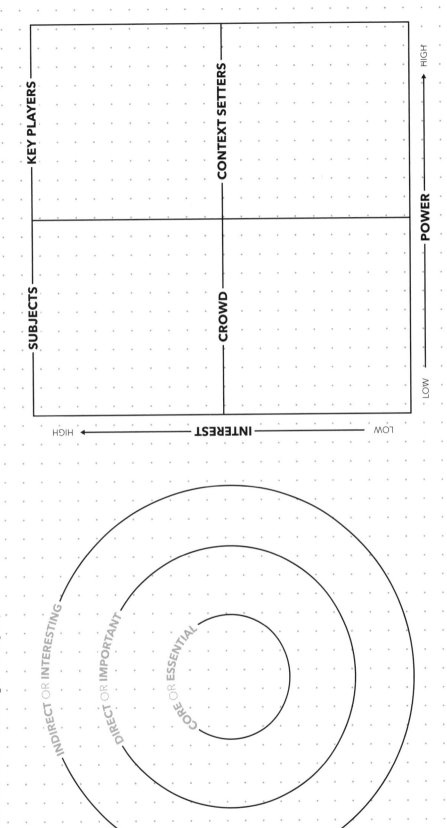

SUBJECTS — KEY PLAYERS

CROWD — CONTEXT SETTERS

INTEREST (LOW / HIGH)

POWER (LOW / HIGH)

INDIRECT OR INTERESTING

DIRECT OR IMPORTANT

CORE OR ESSENTIAL

BUSINESS MODEL CONTENT ANALYSIS

ANALYSING BUSINESS MODELS TO UNDERSTAND THE COMPETITION

This tool can help you analyse the business models of a range of organisations to identify their distinguishing factors or competitive advantage.

STEP 1: Make a list of all your competitors, then select a manageable number. Write the name of each selected organisation in the left column.

STEP 2: Select a set of criteria for analysis and indicate these in the top row (for our recommended criteria see pg. 72).

STEP 3: Work your way through the columns for each organisation by searching for information online.

COMPANY NAME	CRITERIA 1	CRITERIA 2	CRITERIA 3	CRITERIA 4	CRITERIA 5	CRITERIA 6

CUSTOMER SEGMENT PROFILES

BREAKING THINGS INTO SMALLER PARTS TO GAIN INSIGHTS

Firms will often give a descriptive nickname to their market segments. A well-known example of a nickname is 'baby boomers', which refers to the generation of people born after 1945 up until the early 1960s. Subsequent generations are now referred to as Generation X, Gen Y and now Generation Z. The purpose of a nickname is to quickly identify and understand the market segment inside the firm when discussing it in reports, presentations and meetings. This activity is intended to be completed after SEGMENTING CUSTOMERS. **Work through the main sections, filling in each one to represent your chosen markets, then develop one persona which represents each market segment.**

SEGMENT NICKNAME: ....

—— SEGMENT SIZE MEASURES ——

—— PORTION OF THE OVERALL MARKET ——

—— MAIN CONSUMER NEEDS ——

—— PRODUCT INVOLVEMENT LEVELS ——

—— RETAILER PREFERENCES ——

—— GEOGRAPHIC SPREAD ——

—— DEMOGRAPHIC DESCRIPTION ——

—— PSYCHOGRAPHIC DESCRIPTION ——

—— USAGE LEVEL ——

—— LEVEL OF BRAND LOYALTY ——

—— PRICE SENSITIVITY ——

—— EXAMPLE PERSONA OF MARKET SEGMENT ——

NAME:

AGE:

GENDER:

INCOME:

EDUCATION:

SOCIAL STATUS:

FAMILY:

LIFE STAGE:

OCCUPATION:

—— PHOTO ——

—— MAIN COMPETITIVE OFFERINGS ——

—— MAIN MEDIA CHOICES ——

DESIGN INNOVATION & INTEGRATION STRAKER, WRIGLEY & NUSEM 2020

MARKET DISRUPTORS

Throughout history there have been many "game changers" to most markets. This activity requires you think of a major disruptor to a number of different markets. There is no limitation of the era or type of disruption you choose as long as you can provide an explanation for it.

STEP 1: Go through each of the markets below and find an example (product, company, service) which you think has created a disruption. Place a picture/name of the disruptor.

STEP 2: Indicate how and when it disrupted the industry and what you think the cause of the disruption was (e.g. social need, change in laws, technology, science advancement etc.).

MEDICAL	ENERGY	ADULT INDUSTRY	HOSPITALITY	COMMUNICATIONS	INSURANCE

FINANCIAL SERVICES	BUSINESS SERVICES	CONSUMER SERVICES	TRANSPORTATION	TRAVEL	CONSUMER PRODUCTS

RETAIL	ENTERTAINMENT	FOOD/BEVERAGE	HEALTH	MASS MEDIA	BUILDING/CONSTRUCTION

NON-PROFIT	EDUCATION	MANUFACTURING	TECHNOLOGY	LEGAL	AUTOMOTIVE

BUSINESS MODEL SWOT

Complete this tool after the BUSINESS MODEL ANALYSIS.

Step 1: Identify four companies or business typologies and write their names in the first column.

Step 2: Continue to fill in the remaining columns for each company. For the last column, identify a distinguishing factor which a company could take advantage of and explain how (e.g. another company's weakness might be your strength —which you might be able to capitalise on).

COMPANY NAME	STRENGTH	WEAKNESS	THREAT	OPPORTUNITY	DISTINGUISHING FACTOR

PLOT THE COMPETITION

STEP 1: Decide on what axes your sector could be compared (e.g. on the continuums of quality, price, market share, customer satisfaction, etc.). It is recommended that you pick two dimensions that are tailored to your context. We've provided two templates so that you can explore different combinations.

STEP 2: Assign one dimension to the horizontal axis (so that the left-hand side represents one extreme and the right-hand side represents the other – e.g. low cost and high cost). Do the same for the vertical axis but with a different dimension.

STEP 3: Place the name or logo of the companies you have analysed on the matrix according to their fit. Provide justification for you placement of each company. Tip: empty (white) space represents a gap in the market that you could take advantage of.

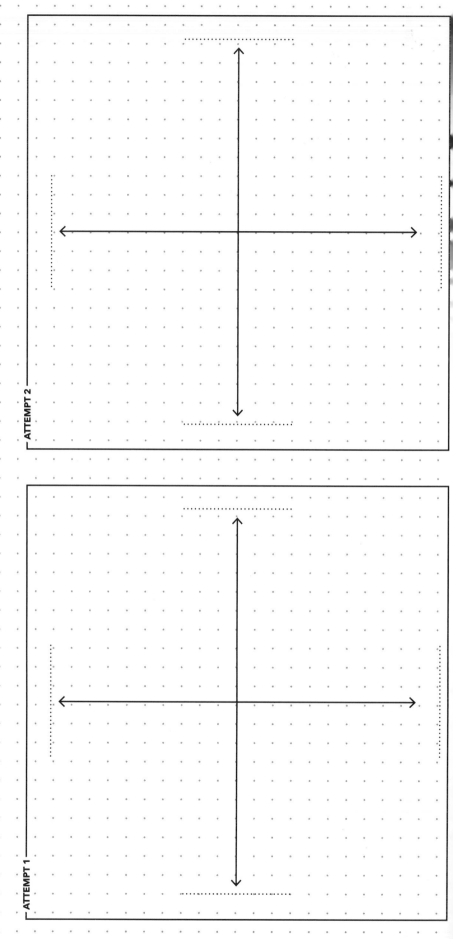

ATTEMPT 1

ATTEMPT 2

DESIGN INNOVATION & INTEGRATION STRAKER, WRIGLEY & NUSEM 2020

SEGMENTING CUSTOMERS

STEP 1: The first step in selecting a market segment is defining your market. Indicate your market in the top row.

STEP 2: Identify sub-markets. List a number of sub-markets that fit into the chosen market in the second row.

STEP 3: Create market segments in the third row and below. Determine what types (segments) of different customers form one sub-market. These could be separated by demographic, geographic, behavioural and or psychographic segments.

DESIGN INNOVATION & INTEGRATION STRAKER, WRIGLEY & NUSEM 2020

PRODUCT ANALYSIS

STEP 1: ANALYSE THE COMPETITION

- The easiest way is to search for items similar to yours, and to search amazon.com or similar for reviews (if the product is for consumers).
- The best way to learn about competitors is ask your potential customers (if possible).
- Consider substitutes, look-alikes, and doing nothing.
- You could use the competitor SWOT and data sheet templates, or create your own / similar to the one in the example (see pg.73).

STEP 2: CONSIDER REGULATORY OR CERTIFICATION ISSUES

- What permits, certifications or regulatory clearances will your product need?
- What agency or organisation issues them?
- How long does the process take?
- How much is it likely to cost – for filing the permit and the testing to collect key data?

STEP 3: NOTICE MARKET TRENDS

- While doing your research, what do you notice about the industry/market?
- What are the major concerns or opportunities being discussed?
- How receptive is your industry to new innovations?
- Is the industry crowded with new competitors?
- What are the implications for you?

VALUE DEFINITION

KNOWING YOUR 'WHY'

The value definition tool can help an organisation understand its 'why', and to frame a new and compelling 'why' in the form of a value proposition. This is accomplished through a set of guided questions which examine an organisation's 'what', 'how' and 'why', and then consider these elements again in the reverse order. The same is then done from a customer's perspective. This can help highlight discrepancies between what the organisation does and what is expected of customers, thus framing a new value proposition.

STEP 1: Fill out the LEFT-hand side from the perspective of the ORGANISATION.

STEP 2: Fill out the RIGHT-hand side from the perspective of the CUSTOMER.

1) WHAT DOES YOUR ORGANISATION DO?

1) WHAT DOES YOUR CUSTOMER THINK THE ORGANISATION DOES?

2) HOW DOES YOUR ORGANISATION PERFORM ITS KEY ACTIVITIES?

2) HOW DOES YOUR CUSTOMER THINK THE ORGANISATION PERFORMS ITS KEY ACTIVITIES?

3) WHY DOES YOUR ORGANISATION PERFORM THESE ACTIVITIES?

3) WHY DOES YOUR CUSTOMER CHOOSE YOU OVER YOUR COMPETITOR(S)?

4) WHY DOES THE ORGANISATION DO WHAT IT DOES?

4) WHY VALUE DO YOU PROVIDE TO YOUR CUSTOMER?

5) HOW DOES THE ORGANISATION ACHIEVE THIS?

5) HOW DOES YOUR CUSTOMER KNOW ABOUT THIS VALUE?

6) WHAT CHANGES DOES THE ORGANISATION NEED TO DO TO REINFORCE THE WHY?

6) WHAT CHANGES ARE NEEDED SO YOUR CUSTOMER KNOWS YOUR VALUE?

DESIGN BRIEF

FRAMING YOUR DESIGN INTENTIONS TO MEET CUSTOMER NEEDS

This tool can be used to help frame the direction for design. It will assist you to determine what the outcomes and direction of design should be (not what the actual design should be). **Simply list the motivations, rules and criteria required, along with any problems or organisational constraints that should be taken into account.**

PROJECT BRIEF: ....

PREPARED BY: ....

Outlines the customer latent needs and frames the design intent in order to guide ideation and solution development.

FRAME DESIGN INTENT

Describe what problem customers are having and what they want to achieve?
What are their requirements, expectations and desires for solving this problem?

DESIGN CONSIDERATIONS AND CONSTRAINTS

What are the rules and criteria for a successful concept?
What are must haves involved in an appropriate solution?
What are the potential constraints of the solution (e.g. manufacturing costs, user behaviours)?

DESIGN INNOVATION & INTEGRATION STRAKER, WRIGLEY & NUSEM 2020

DEFINING YOUR PHILOSOPHY

UNDERSTANDING WHAT YOU VALUE AS A DESIGNER

DESIGN INNOVATION & INTEGRATION STRAKER, WRIGLEY & NUSEM 2020

Design principles, as explained in the book, are a set of philosophical rules that guide design practice. This tool can help you define your design principles. To complete the tool work through the steps outlined in the in the DESIGN Component (see pg. 110), then follow the steps below.

Step 1: State your design principle by writing the name of it in the first column. Alternatively, you can frame principles as statements which explain what design means to you and how you wish to practice it (e.g., the design principle of 'sustainability' could be used to communicate your passion for the environment and desire to positively impact it).

Step 2: In the box next to each principle clearly describe what the principle entails.

DESIGN PRINCIPLE NAME	DESCRIPTION

VISUALISE YOUR PRACTICE

DESCRIBE YOUR DESIGN PRACTICE VISUALLY

Think about your 'process' for design, define it and then describe it visually in the space below.

YOUR DEFINITION OF DESIGN: ....

DESIGN INNOVATION & INTEGRATION| STRAKER, WRIGLEY & NUSEM 2020

DESIGN CRITERIA

DESIGN INNOVATION & INTEGRATION STRAKER, WRIGLEY & NUSEM 2020

As explained in the book design criteria can be divided into primary and secondary criteria.

STEP 1: Start by giving each criteria a catchy name (place in the first column of boxes).

STEP 2: Provide a short description of each criteria (fill in the second column of boxes).

STEP 3: Classify them either as primary or secondary criterion (final column of boxes).

CRITERIA NAME	DESCRIPTION	PRIMARY OR SECONDARY

SOLUTION EVALUATION

Diagramming to think through solutions and to show how solutions work. The purpose of this tool is to visually, quickly and easily benchmark multiple design solutions and evaluate how well they meet your intent and the criteria set.

STEP 1: List your criteria in the first column and sketch each of your solutions in the boxes in the first row.

STEP 2: For each solution, go through the criteria and (in the space next to each criterion) provide a short explanation of how it (or how it doesn't) meet the defined criterion.

STEP 3: Once each solution has been critiqued add notes on how it could be adjusted to fulfil any criteria that were not met.

CRITERIA

SOLUTION 1

ADJUSTMENT

SOLUTION 2

ADJUSTMENT

SOLUTION 3

ADJUSTMENT

DESIGNING INNOVATIVE PRODUCTS

DESIGN INNOVATION & INTEGRATION STRAKER, WRIGLEY & NUSEM 2020

This tool is based off the Ansoff Directional Policy Matrix.

STEP 1: Choose the company you want to work for.

STEP 2: Choose and write the name of product that is currently available and the market it is targeted at. Sketch the product it in the first square. Make notes of key features.

STEP 3: Move to the next square, write down the new market you have selected and sketch a new product design that fits the descriptor. Make notes of key features.

STEP 4: Continue the same steps for square 3 and 4.

CURRENT PRODUCT: ....

CURRENT MARKET: ....

NEW PRODUCT: ....

CURRENT MARKET: ....

CURRENT PRODUCT: ....

NEW MARKET: ....

NEW PRODUCT: ....

NEW MARKET: ....

CIRCLE CREATION.

Draw as many objects as you can using the circles below (these could be natural or human-made designs). The designs must not strictly adhere to a circle. You can add to the circle or use multiple circles in one design. The most creative design wins!

DESIGN INNOVATION & INTEGRATION. STRAKER, WRIGLEY & NUSEM 2020

INNOVATION MASHING

This tool was designed by IDEO (https://www.ideou.com/pages/ideation-method-mash-up). To complete, follow the instructions at the top of each column.

CATEGORY 1: Write down the key elements in your opportunity context (e.g. banking experience - which might include waiting in line at the bank).

CATEGORY 2: Write down the key elements in a completely different context/experience (e.g., things that you would find in a hotel room - like a Mini-bar).

CATEGORY 3: Randomly combine category 1 and 2, providing a description for each (for instance, '1A' 'Bank Mini-bar a fridge filled with cold drinks while you wait).

1:
2:
3:
4:
5:
6:
7:
8:
9:
10:
11:
12:
13:
14:
15:
16:
17:
18:
19:
20:

A:
B:
C:
D:
E:
F:
G:
H:
I:
J:
K:
L:
M:
N:
O:
P:
Q:
R:
S:
T:

1A:

MR SQUIGGLE

Anybody remember (the slightly creepy but) very popular kids show in Australia in the 90s Mr. Squiggle?

If you don't, Mr. Squiggle was a puppet that would turn random lines and shapes into recognisable images using his pencil nose. This is a simple and fun activity to 'warm-up' your creative brain. Use the random lines and shapes to form images. The aim is to be as creative as you can!

POST-IT NOTE PICTIONARY

Yes! Just like the classic game Pictionary, but a little bit harder by restricting you to the space of a Post-it Note. Grab some post-it notes or copies of this template, a timer (this could be your phone), some pens and a big list of random things (e.g., movies, countries, a random word generator from Google, etc.). This is a fun warm-up activity to practice visual thinking.

STEP 1: Sit so everyone can see each other, then give each person a word (make sure that only you see your word – don't show anyone else what it is).

STEP 2: Take a moment to think about how you can use only images (no letters or numbers) to communicate what that word is.

STEP 3: In turns, each person will have 30 seconds to draw their word while the rest of the group guesses what it is.

STEP 4: After each turn fill in the question under the 'post-it notes.'

NAME OF ARTIST:

CORRECTLY GUESSED: ☐ YES ☐ NO

TIME OF SUCCESSFUL GUESS:

WORD:

NAME OF ARTIST:

CORRECTLY GUESSED: ☐ YES ☐ NO

TIME OF SUCCESSFUL GUESS:

WORD:

NAME OF ARTIST:

CORRECTLY GUESSED: ☐ YES ☐ NO

TIME OF SUCCESSFUL GUESS:

WORD:

LETTERS AND NUMBERS

Don't you wish you could write like a designer?! This very simply tool will make you take a conscious approach to how you are writing letters and numbers. Start by tracing over the letters and numbers; do this until you have perfected it; or you have created your own, unique style of font!

DESIGN INNOVATION & INTEGRATION STRAKER, WRIGLEY & NUSEM 2020

PROTOTYPE PLAN

EMBODYING CONCEPTS IN TANGIBLE FORMS TO GET FEEDBACK FROM USERS

STEP 1: Identify concepts to be prototyped. Review concepts to identify those that will benefit most from testing in tangible form. Determine the kinds of readily available materials you will need to create a rough embodiment of the concept. Determine what kind of prototype – appearance prototype, performance prototype, or a combination of both – will be most useful at that stage of the process.

STEP 2: Create a prototyping space and build to learn. It is a good idea to identify or create a space where your team can build and test concept prototypes. Assemble the kinds of materials and tools you will use for building, modifying and testing prototypes.

STEP 3: Review prototypes, test and discuss. Present concept prototypes to your team in a review session and to a group of users. Test these prototypes and discuss each one in light of the stated design principles, user needs, form factors, human factors and other dimensions. How does it feel to hold the prototype? Is it intuitive? Comfortable? Does it make sense? Generate insights about refinements to the core concept. The review is also an opportunity to explore alternative concepts, consider combinations of features from different prototypes, and get guidance for iteration.

STEP 4: Modify prototypes and iterate. Build on existing prototypes, modify them, or create new ones to reflect input gathered through the review process. Iterate and continue to incorporate feedback into the prototype.

STEP 5: Summarise key learning. Use the conclusion of the review sessions to record the key learning and results from testing. Summarise how the prototype evolved from an initial manifestation to a final desired state. Share this information among team members and stakeholders to reinforce decisions about further development.

DESCRIBE THE DEVELOPMENT OF THE IDEA AND WHAT PARTS OF IT NEED TO BE TESTED AND WHY

Briefly describe what you will test. Answer at least the following questions: For whom? What? How? You can use both words and illustrations in your answer.

PLANNING THE TEST

RESOURCES: What is required to test the idea quickly with potential customers?

INVESTMENTS: What are the projected expenses for the test? E.g. 20 hours of work, team roles, etc.

MEASURES AND OBSERVATION: What measures and means will be used to determine the success and failures of the test?

PITCHING

SHOWING AND TELLING OTHERS WHY YOUR SOLUTION IS THE BEST!

STEP 1: WRITE YOUR SOLUTION IN ONE SENTENCE

STEP 2: ILLUSTRATE THIS SENTENCE ONLY USING IMAGES

STEP 3: WRITE A TITLE AND SUPPORTING PHRASE FOR THE INNOVATION

Create a distinctive and compelling title for the proposed innovation. Just as in a slogan, using a few words write a short supporting phrase to concisely express the essence of the innovation.

STEP 4: WRITE SHORT DESCRIPTIONS OF CHALLENGES AND SOLUTIONS

Write a short description about the challenges (problems) being addressed by your project. In parallel, write about how the innovation solutions respond to these challenges and what benefits (value) they bring.

PROBLEM

SOLUTION

PRODUCT CLASSIFICATION MATRIX

Select 10 different products and place them on the classification matrix, provide a justification for your decision.

LIST YOUR PRODUCTS

	NEW CORE PRODUCT	NEXT GENERATION PRODUCT	ADDITION TO PRODUCT FAMILY	DERIVATIVES AND ENHANCEMENTS	**JUSTIFICATION**
BREAKTHROUGH					EXPLAIN YOUR CLASSIFICATION SELECTION FOR EACH PRODUCT
NEW CORE PROCESS		**PLATFORM PRODUCTS**			
NEXT GENERATION PROCESS					
UPGRADE				**INCREMENTAL PRODUCTS**	
INCREMENTAL CHANGE					

3 HORIZONS

The three horizons model details how things are done now (Horizon 1 / H1 - business as usual), the future model (Horizon 3 / H3) and the transitional activities that will be required to progress between these two states (Horizon 2 / H2). For more information see Sharpe et al. (2016).

Step 1: Examine present concerns by detailing the faults of the current state of things.

Step 2: Explore future aspirations by conceiving aspirational possibilities for the future (that will supersede the state in the first step).

Step 3: Detail any current inspirational practices (these are examples of emerging innovations).

Step 4: Spot any innovations that are emerging in response to failings of the current state or opportunities from the aspirational future state.

Step 5: Identify the essential features in current systems that must be maintained in the future.

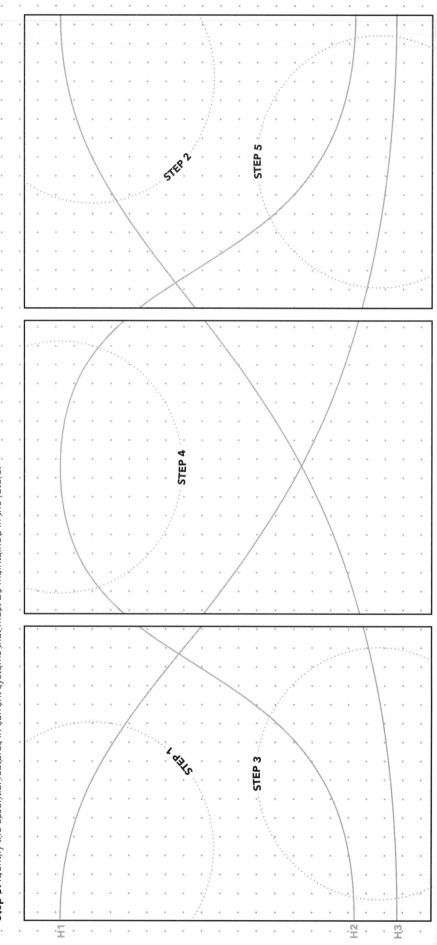

JOHNSON & JONES MATRIX

The Johnson and Jones Matrix can help you explore multiple ideas (design concepts) through ideation. This is accomplished by re-designing concepts through the prompts inside each cell in the canvas below. By pushing the boundaries with your design piece-by-piece you increase the chances to radically change your idea. In this instance, by simultaneously increasing the market newness and the technology newness.

STEP 1: Follow the prompts below, starting in the top left-hand corner and working your way to the bottom right-hand corner – iterate your design based on these prompts in each cell.

STEP 2: Evaluate the concepts to determine which you should proceed with.

INCREASING TECHNOLOGY NEWNESS

Product objectives	No technological change	Improved technology	New technology to acquire scientific knowledge and production skills new to the company
No market change	Sustain	Reformulation to maintain optimum balance of cost, quality, availability in formula of present products	Replacement to seek new and better ingredients of formulation for present company products in technology not employed
Strengthened market to exploit more fully existing markets for present competitor's products	Remerchandising to increase sales to consumers of types now served by the company	Improved product to improve present products for greater utility and merchantability to consumers	Product line extension to broaden the line of products offered to present consumers through new technology
New market to increase the number of types of consumers served by the company	New use to find new classes of consumer that can utilise present company products	Market extension to reach new class of consumer by modifying present products	Diversification to add to the classes of consumer served by developing new technology knowledge

← INCREASING MARKET NEWNESS →

DESIGN CATALYST

This canvas can be used to evaluate your characteristics and skill-sets as a design catalyst. The canvas can also be used by organisations as a basis for writing a job description for a design catalyst, thus ensuring that an appropriate candidate is selected.

STEP 1: Answer the questions posed in each box. These will explore your role inside an organisation and the skills required to perform it. Make sure to start with 'Catalyst Value'.

STEP 2: Circle any points in the lists starting with 'e.g.' that you have not detailed in your responses to the questions. These are areas for improvement.

DESIGN INNOVATION & INTEGRATION: STRAKER, WRIGLEY & NUSEM 2020

HELPERS

Who helps you provide and deliver this value?

Who should you keep in the inner and outer circles?

E.g. industry networks, university alumni, other DCs, researchers, design champions, industry sponsors, government agencies, etc.

ACTIONS

What you do on a daily basis to reinforce your value?

What critical activities do you perform to distinguish you from others, and to showcase and disseminate your design knowledge?

E.g. design tools, teach tools, disseminate knowledge, generate insights, question assumptions, etc.

CHARACTERISTICS

Who are you and what makes you different?

E.g. positivist leader, design skills, inquisitive mind, reflective nature, entrepreneurial, collect and collate research findings, analyse and devise process to innovate, thirst for knowledge, driven by innovation, etc.

CATALYST VALUE

How do you help?

What expertise do you bring to help drive innovation?

E.g. new customer insights, designing new business models, build and communicate business offerings, link and unite separated parts of the business, understand the future customer, agitate purposefully), distribute knowledge, etc.

SKILLS

What expertise do you require?

What unique skills do you have to deliver this value?

E.g. Visualisation skills, problem solving skills, co-design skills, convergent and divergent thinking, customer journey mapping, ability to empathise, interpersonal, group facilitation, mediating, questioning, etc.

INSTRUMENTS

How do you deliver value?

E.g. networking events, co-design workshops, group facilitation, personal relationships, build rapport, meaningful conversations, embedded practice, outside in perspective, conferences, etc.

DELIVERY

Who do you help?

Who benefits form your efforts?

E.g. industry partners, suppliers, customers, project leaders, etc.

DESIGN CATALYST CAPABILITIES

DESIGN INNOVATION & INTEGRATION STRAKER, WRIGLEY & NUSEM 2020

This tool can be used to rank your design innovation capabilities and help you determine which areas you could improve in.

STEP 1: Determine how confident you are with each of the capabilities on the hexagon below (rule breaker, research rigour, business acumen, design intuition, customer-centred and agile facilitation).

STEP 2: Assign a grade for each dimension on a scale of 1-5 (with 1 being weak and 5 being strong).

STEP 3: Draw a line between each corner of the hexagon to show your strengths and weaknesses, this will highlight what skills you may wish to develop. You can also overlay your shape with other team members to see what skills your team is lacking and what areas you are strong in.

RULE BREAKER

How confident are you in re-framing problems that challenge organisational assumptions surrounding product problems and constraints, procedural processes?

BUSINESS ACUMEN

How confident are you in leading an organisational change process and transformation?

CUSTOMER-CENTRED

How confident are you with empathising with customers and collecting customer insights?

RESEARCH RIGOUR

How confident are you at investigating, synthesising, critiquing and interpreting data into useful applications in the organisation?

DESIGN INTUITION

How confident are you in visualising, translating ideas, prototyping concepts and business models?

AGILE FACILITATION

How confident are you in your own design practice and facilitating an impromptu practice with others?

ORGANISATIONAL CONDITION AUDIT

DESIGN INNOVATION & INTEGRATION (STRAKER, WRIGLEY & NUSEM 2020)

GAUGING ALIGNMENT OF CONDITIONS BETWEEN FRONT-LINE AND EXECUTIVE STAFF

STEP 1: Collect data from front-line and executive staff about the organisational conditions (e.g. through interviews or informal conversation).

STEP 2: Plot the data into each cell, then compare front-line and executive perspectives to find alignment (or misalignment) surrounding the organisational conditions.

	STRATEGIC VISION	DIRECTIVE(S)	FACILITIES	CULTURAL CAPITAL
FRONT-LINE	How do front-line staff describe the organisation's vision? What do they think of it?	Are the organisation's staff aware of any (non-role specific) design directive(s)?	What spaces and resources do front-line staff believe are available to assist them in conducting their roles?	Do front-line staff believe they are supported (e.g. receive sufficient training and support) to perform non-role specific directives (such as practicing design)? Are they aware of design's value?
EXECUTIVE	How do the organisation's executive describe its vision? Do they embody this vision? If so, through what actions?	What design directives(s) do the organisation's executive team believe staff are following?	What spaces and resources do executives believe have been provided to staff to assist them in conducting their roles and design?	What efforts have been taken by the executive team to communicate the value of key initiatives (such as design practice) and to ensure that staff acquire the requisite skills to follow directive(s)?
ALIGNMENT	Is there a shared understanding of the organisation's vision between its front-line staff and executives? What could be done to achieve a better alignment?	Is there consensus about directive(s) between the organisation's front-line staff and executive? How could a consensus be reached?	Are the available facilities and resources well known, understood and accessible from both parties' perspectives? How could these facilities and resources become better known and accessed?	Are perceptions of training and initiatives to support the organisation's core mandates aligned across front-line and executive staff? How could the need for such initiatives be identified, and the initiatives implemented?

ORGANISATIONAL CONDITION MATRIX

DESIGN INNOVATION & INTEGRATION STRAKER, WRIGLEY & NUSEM 2020

DETERMINING HOW THE ORGANISATIONAL CONDITIONS CAN BE IMPROVED

STEP 1: Fill in the numbered cells to evaluate the current organisational conditions (#1, 3, 5 & 7), along with why that is the case and how it can be improved (#2, 4, 6 & 8).

STEP 2: Fill in the remaining cells to determine how each condition could be leveraged to improve another. The questions are structured so that the organisational condition listed in the rows are framed as the lead for improving the ones listed in the columns.

	STRATEGIC VISION	DIRECTIVE(S)	FACILITIES	CULTURAL CAPITAL
STRATEGIC VISION • Does the organisation have a vision (aim/mission) for the future? • Does the organisation have appetite for change or innovation?	**1** Why is the organisation's vision what it is? How can this vision better align to stakeholder needs?	How can the organisation's vision be used to inform the directive(s) given to staff?	How can the organisation's vision be reflected in the spaces and resources it provides?	How can the organisation's vision be communicated to its people?
DIRECTIVE(S) • Are the organisation's people held accountable in practicing design? • Are there key performance indicators which detail design practice? • Are there roles in the organisation which reflect design practice?	**2** How can the organisation leverage its directives to exemplify its vision?	**3** What is the rationale behind the organisation's current directive(s)? Are there mechanisms ensuring these directive(s) are followed?	How can the organisation leverage its directive(s) to improve its environment?	How can the organisation's directive(s) be used to shape its cultural capital?
FACILITIES • Is design given a space within the organisation? • Are the required resources for design provided?	How can the organisation's spaces and resources reinforce its vision?	**4** How can the organisation better equip its people (through resources and spaces) to follow the directive(s) given?	**5** Why are the organisation's facilities the way they are? How can they be improved?	How can the organisation's facilities best serve its people?
CULTURAL CAPITAL • Does the organisation have a vision for the future? • Does the organisation have appetite for change or innovation?	How can the organisation's cultural capital help to frame its vision?	How can the organisation's people be supported to follow the directive(s) given?	**6** How can the organisation's cultural capital inform the design of its spaces and the acquisition of resources?	**7** Why is the organisation's cultural capital in its current state and composition? Does it reflect the organisation's needs?

8

THINKING STYLES

Using this template and the steps outlined in the book (see pg. 184) you can use the thinking styles for your own project or brief.

DESIGN THINKING

DESIGN THINKING

CREATIVE THINKING

INTEGRATED THINKING

This model outlines a recommended process for combining the strengths of each thinking style into one approach. The model could be used to help individuals with different thinking styles to work together or by an individual seeking to understand the strengths and weakness of each thinking style. One suggested way of using this model is to map out a current design project (or a planned one) across three stages (conception, development and implementation).

STEP 1: Write the main tasks to complete across the three stages.

STEP 2: Under each of the tasks, write what thinking style would be best suited to complete the task.

STEP 3: For each of the tasks write the name of someone in your project team who is best suited for the task (you might not have anyone capable of completing some tasks, this indicates that you may need to recruit a new team member).

STEP 4: Draw a line to connect all the tasks performed by the same person. Some individuals might be required for the whole project, and others only for a particular stage.

──── CONCEPTION ────

──── DEVELOPMENT ────

──── IMPLEMENTATION ────

REFERENCES

Adams, J. (1974). Conceptual blockbusting. Stanford, CA: Stanford Alumni Association.

Almeida, L. S., Prieto, L. P., Ferrando, M., Oliveira, E., & Ferrándiz, C. (2008). Torrance Test of Creative Thinking: The question of its construct validity. Thinking Skills and Creativity, 3(1), 53-58.

Ansoff, H. I. (1957). Strategies for diversification. Harvard business review, 35(5), 113-124.

Archer, L. & Bruce. (1967) Design Management, Management Decision 1.4: 47–51.

Armstrong, S. J., Cools, E., & Sadler Smith, E. (2012). Role of cognitive styles in business and management: Reviewing 40 years of research. International Journal of Management Reviews, 14(3), 238-262.

Arnold, J. (1956). Problem solving—A creative approach (National Defence University, Publication No. L57-20). Washington, DC: Industrial College of the Armed Forces.

Asimow, M. (1962). Introduction to Design. Englewood Cliffs, NJ: Prentice-Hall.

Assink, M. (2006). Inhibitors of disruptive innovation capability: a conceptual model. Management, 9(2), 215-233.

Beckman, S. & Barry, M. (2007). Innovation as a learning process: Embedding design thinking, California management review, 50(1), 25-56.

Beckman, S. & Barry, M. (2008). Developing Design Thinking Capabilities. Academic Research Library, 24(82).

Bennett, A. (2011). Design Integrations: Research and Collaboration. Design and Culture, 3(1), 123-125.

Berkun, S. (2010). The myths of innovation. O'Reilly Media, Inc.

Best, K. (2015). Design Management. Managing Design Strategy, Process and Implementation (2nd ed.). London: Fairchild Books.

Borja de Mozota, B. (2002). Design and competitive edge: A model for design management excellence in European SMEs 1. Academic Review, 2(1), 88-103.

Boztepe, S. (2007). User value: Competing theories and models. International journal of design, 1(2).

Broeck, H.V.D., Vanderheyden, K. and Cools, E. (2003). The field of cognitive styles: from a theoretical review to the construction of the cognitive style inventory. Working Paper Series 2003/26, Vlerick Leuven Gent Management School, Gent, Belgium.

Brown, T. (2009). Change by Design: How Design Thinking Transforms Organizations and Inspires Innovation, Harper Business.

Brown, T. (2008). Design thinking. Harvard business review, 86(6), 84–92.

Bruce, M., & Bessant, J. R. (2002). Design in business: Strategic innovation through design. Pearson education.

Bryson, J. (2003). What to do when stakeholders matter: A guide to stakeholder identification and analysis techniques Public and Nonprofit Strategic Management View project. National Public Management Research Conference.

Buchanan, R. (1992). Wicked Problems in Design Thinking, Design Issues, 8(2), 5–21.

Buchanan, R. (1995). Rhetoric, Humanism, and Design, in Buchanan, R. & Margolin, V. (eds.), Discovering Design: Exploration in Design Studies, University of Chicago Press, Chicago, 23-66.

Buchanan, R. (2001). Design Research and the New Learning, Design Issues, 17(4), 3-23.

Bucolo, S., & Matthews, J. H. (2011). Design led innovation: Exploring the synthesis of needs, technologies and business models. In Proceedings of Participatory Interaction Conference 2011.

Cagan, J. & Vogel, C. (2002). Creating breakthrough products: Innovation from product planning to program approval. Ft Press. What Things Mean. Cambridge: Harvard Business Press.

Calabretta, G., & Gemser, G. (2015). Integrating design into the fuzzy front end of the innovation process. Design thinking: New product development essentials from the PDMA, 105-124.

Carlgren, L., Elmquist, M., & Rauth, I. (2016). The challenges of using design thinking in industry—experiences from five large firms. Creativity and Innovation Management, 25(3), 344-362.

Chatterjee, N. (2009). A study of organisational culture and its effect on employee retention. ASBM Journal of Management, 2(2), 147–155.

Chesbrough, H. (2010). Business model innovation: opportunities and barriers. Long range planning, 43(2-3), 354-363.

Chitturi, R., Raghunathan, R. & Mahajan, V. (2008). Delight by Design: The Role of Hedonic Versus Utilitarian Benefits. American Marketing Association, 72, 48–63.

Cooper, R., Junginger, S., & Lockwood, T. (Eds.). (2013). The handbook of design management. A&C Black.

Coulson-Thomas, C. (1992). Strategic vision or strategic con?: Rhetoric or reality?. Long range planning, 25(1), 81-89.

Cross, N. (1982). Designerly ways of knowing. Design studies, 3(4), 221-227.

Cross, N. (2006). Designerly Ways of Knowing. Dordrecht.: Springer-Verlag.

Cross, N. (2011). Design Thinking: Understanding How Designers Think and Work. New York: Berg.

d.school. (2010). An introduction to design thinking. Process guide, Stanford University.

Daly, P., & Davy, D. (2015). Crafting the Investor Pitch Using Insights from Rhetoric and Linguistics. In G. M. Alessi & G. Jacobs (Eds.), The Ins and Outs of Business and Professional Discourse Research: Reflections on Interacting with the Workplace (pp. 182–203). London: Palgrave McMillan.

Davidsson, P. (2003). The domain of entrepreneurship research: Some suggestions. Advances in entrepreneurship, firm emergence and growth, 6(3), 315-372.

De Bono, E. (1989) Six thinking hats. London: Penguin.

De Bont, C., & Liu, S. X. (2017). Breakthrough Innovation through Design Education: Perspectives of Design-Led Innovators. Design Issues, 33(2), 18-30.

De Jong, C.W. (2017). Dieter Rams:Ten Principles for Good Design. Prestel:UK

Dean, G., Fahsing, I.A., Gottschalk, P., Solli-Saether, H. (2008). Investigative thinking and creativity: an empirical study of police detectives in Norway. International Journal of Innovation and Learning, 5(2), 170-185.

Dearlove, D. (2006). Inside the innovation lab. Business. Strategy Review, Spring, 5–8.

Dong, A. (2015). Design× innovation: perspective or evidence-based practices. International Journal of Design Creativity and Innovation, 3(3-4), 148-163.

Dorst, K. (2006). Design Problems and Design Paradoxes. Design Issues, 22(3): 4-14

Dorst, K. (2011). The core of 'design thinking' and its application. Design Studies, 32(6), 521-532.

Dorst, K. (2012). Frame Innovation: Create new thinking by design. Cambridge, MA: MIT Press.

Dorst, K. (2015). Frame innovation: Create new thinking by design. MIT press.

Dorst, K., & Cross, N. (2001). Creativity in the Design Process: Co-evolution of problem-solution. Design Studies, 22(5), 425-437.

Drews, C. (2009). Unleashing the full Potential of Design Thinking as a Business Method. Design Management Journal, 20(3), 38-44.

Dubin, J. (2018). Four types of failure you can (and should) avoid. The Startup. Medium. Retrieved from https://medium.com/

Dunne, D., Martin, R & Rotman, J. (2006). Design Thinking and How It Will Change Management Education: An Interview and Discussion, The Academy of Management Learning and Education, 5(4).

Ensici, A., Badke-Schaub, P., Bayaz t, N., & Lauche, K. (2013). Used and rejected decisions in design teamwork. CoDesign, 9(2), 113-131.

Erlhoff, M., & Marshall, T. (Eds.). (2007). Design dictionary: perspectives on design terminology. Walter de Gruyter.

Evans, M. (2011). Empathizing with the Future : Creating. The Design Journal, 14(2).

Freeman, R. E. (1984). Strategic management: A stakeholder approach. Strategic Management: A Stakeholder Approach. Marshfield, Massachusetts: Pitman.

Ghobadi, M., Shoghi, B. (2013). The effect of thinking styles on the organizational innovation in the metal industry city in Iran Kaveh. International Journal of Basic and Applied Sciences, 2(4), 128-133.

Guilford, J. (1950). Creativity. American Psychologist, 5, 444–454.

Gulledge, T. (2006). What is integration. Industrial Management & Data Systems, 106(1), 5-20.

Hayes, J. R. (1989). Cognitive processes in creativity. In Handbook of creativity, Springer, 135-145.

Henderson, R. M., & Clark, K. B. (1990). Architectural innovation: the reconfiguration of existing product technologies and the failure of established firms. Administrative science quarterly, 9-30.

Hodgkinson, M. (2002). A shared strategic vision: Dream or reality?. The Learning Organization, 9(2), 89–95.

Hokanson, B. (2012). The design critique as a model for distributed learning. In The next generation of distance education, Springer, Boston, MA, 71-83.

Holloway, M. (2009). How tangible is your strategy? How design thinking can turn your strategy into reality. Journal of Business Strategy, 30(2/3), 50-56.

Hultink, E. J., Griffin, A., Hart, S., & Robben, H. S. (1997). Industrial new product launch strategies and product development performance. Journal of product innovation management, 14(4), 243-257.

Ian, W. (1992). Realizing the Power of Strategic Vision. Long Range Planning, 25(5), 18–28.

Isaksen, S. G., & Akkermans, H. J. (2011). Creative Climate: A Leadership Lever for Innovation. The Journal of Creative Behavior, 45(3), 161-187.

Jackson, M. C. (2009). Fifty years of systems thinking for management. Journal of the Operational Research Society, 60(1), S24-S32.

Johnson, G., Scholes, K. & Whittington, R. (2005). Exploring corporate strategy: text and cases. Prentice Hall.

Jones, J. (1970). Design Methods. New York: John Wiley & Sons.

Jones, T. M., & Wicks, A. C. (1999). Convergent stakeholder theory. Academy of management review, 24(2), 206-221.

Joziasse, F., & Selders, T. (2009). The next phase: laying bare the contributions of design. Design Management Review, 20(2), 28-36.

Justice, L. (2019). The Future of Design: Global Product Innovation for a Complex World. Nicholas Brealey Publishing. New York.

Kahn, K. B. (2013). The PDMA handbook of new product development. S. E. Kay, R. Slotegraaf, & S. Uban (Eds.). New York: Wiley.

Keeley, L., Walters, H., Pikkel, R., & Quinn, B. (2013). Ten types of innovation: The discipline of building breakthroughs. John Wiley & Sons.

Kelley, D. & Kelley, T. (2015) Creative Confidence: Unleashing the creative potential within us all. Harper Collins, USA.

Kelley, T. (2001). The Art of Innovation. London: Profile.

Kimbell, L. (2011). Rethinking design thinking: Part I. Design and Culture, 3(3), 285-306.

Koberg, D. & Bagnall, J. (1972). The Universal Traveler: A Soft-Systems Guide to Creativity, Problem-Solving, and the Process of Design. Los Altos, CA: Kaufmann.

Kotler, P. (2003). Marketing insights from A to Z: 80 concepts every manager needs to know. John Wiley & Sons.

Kretzschmar, A. (2003). The Economic Effects of Design, Danish National Agency for Enterprise and Housing. Retrieved from http://www.ebst.dk/file/1924/the_economic_effects_of_designn.pdf

Krippendorff, K. (2006). The Semantic Turn: A New Foundation for Design. CRC Press, Boca Raton, FL.

Kumar, V. (2012) 101 Design Methods: A Structured Approach for Driving Innovation in Your Organization. Hoboken, NJ: Wiley.

Kyffin, S. & Gardien, P. (2009). Navigating the innovation matrix: An approach to design-led innovation. International Journal of Design, 3(1).

Lawson, B. (1980) How Designers Think: The Design Process Demystified. London: Architectural.

Lee, Y., & Evans, D. M. (2012). What Drives Organizations to Employ Design-Driven Approaches? A Study of Fast-Moving Consumer Goods Brand Development. Design Management Journal, 7(1), 74-88.

Leifer, L. (1998). Design-team performance: Metrics and the impact of technology. In S. M. Brown & C. J. Seidner (Eds.), Evaluating corporate training: Models and issues (pp. 297–319). Boston: Kluwer Academic Publishers.

Leifer, L. J., & Steinert, M. (2011). Dancing with ambiguity: Causality behavior, design thinking, and triple-loop-learning. Information Knowledge Systems Management, 10(1-4), 151-173.

Leonard, D., & Sensiper, S. (1998). The role of tacit knowledge in group innovation. California management review, 40(3), 112-132.

Liedtka, J. (2018). Why design thinking works. Harvard Business Review, 96(5), 72-79.

Liedtka, J. & Ogilvie, T. (2011). Designing for growth: A design thinking tool kit for managers. Columbia University Press.

Lloyd, P. & Scott, P. (1994). Discovering the design problem. Design studies, 15(2), 125-140.

Lockwood, T. (2004). Integrating design into organizational culture. Design management review, 15(2), 32-39.

Lockwood, T. (2010) Design Thinking: Integrating Innovation, Customer Experience and Brand Value. New York, New York: Allworth.

Lojacono, G., & Zaccai, G. (2004). The Evolution of the Design-Inspired Enterprise. MIT Sloan Management Review, 45(3), 75–79.

Manzini, E. (2015). Design, when everybody designs: An introduction to design for social innovation. MIT press.

Martin, R. (2007). Design and business: Why can't we be friends. Journal of business Strategy, 28(4), 6-12.

Martin, R. (2009). The Design of Business: Why Design Thinking is the Next Competitive Advantage. Harvard Business Press: Boston.

Martins, E. C., & Terblanche, F. (2003). Building organisational culture that stimulates creativity and innovation. European journal of innovation management.

Maslow, A. (1958). Emotional blocks to creativity. Journal of Individual Psychology, 14(1), 51.

Maslow, A. (1959) New knowledge in Human Values, New York, Harper.

Matthews, J., Bucolo, S., & Wrigley, C. (2012). Challenges and opportunities in the journey of the design-led innovation champions. Paper presented at the Leading Innovation through Design: Proceedings of the DMI 2012 International Research Conference, Boston.

McKim, R. (1973). Experiences in Visual Thinking. Brooks/Cole Publishing Co.

McNeill, T., Gero, J., & Warren, J. (1998). Understanding Conceptual Electronic Design Using Protocol Analysis. Research in Engineering Design, 10(3), 129-140

Mednick, S. (1962). The associative basis of the creative process. Psychological review, 69(3), 220.

Mendelow, A. L. (1981). Environmental Scanning-The Impact of the Stakeholder Concept. In ICIS, 20.

Michalko, M. (2010). Thinkertoys: A handbook of creative-thinking techniques. Ten Speed Press.

Micheli, P., Perks, H., & Beverland, M. B. (2018). Elevating design in the organization. Journal of Product Innovation Management, 35(4), 629-651.

Micheli, P., Wilner, S. J., Bhatti, S. H., Mura, M., & Beverland, M. B. (2019). Doing design thinking: Conceptual review, synthesis, and research agenda. Journal of Product Innovation Management, 36(2), 124-148.

Moore, G. A. (1999). Crossing the chasm (Rev. ed.). New York: Harper Business.

Morris, L. (2009). Business Model Innovation: The Strategy of Business Breakthroughs. International Journal of Innovation Science, 1(4), 191–204.

Moultrie, J., Clarkson, P. J., & Probert, D. (2006). A tool to evaluate design performance in SMEs. International Journal of Productivity and Performance Management, 55(3-4), 184-216.

Mutanen, U.-M. (2008). Developing organisational design capability in a Finland-based engineering corporation: the case of Metso. Design Studies, 29(5), 500–520.

Newman, D. (2019). The design squiggle. Retrieved from https://thedesignsquiggle.com/

Noland, J., & Phillips, R. (2010). Stakeholder engagement, discourse ethics and strategic management. International Journal of Management Reviews, 12(1), 39-49.

Norman, D. (1986) User Centered System Design. Taylor & Francis.

Norman, D. (2010). The Research-Practice Gap: The need for translational developers. Interactions, 9-12.

Norman, D. (1988). The psychology of everyday things. Basic books.

Norman, D. (1999). Affordance, conventions, and design. interactions, 6(3), 38-43.

Norman, D. & Verganti, R. (2014). Incremental and radical innovation: Design research vs. technology and meaning change. Design issues, 30(1), 78-96.

Nusem, E., Matthews, J., & Wrigley, C. (2019). Toward design orientation and integration: Driving design from awareness to action. Design Issues, 35(3), 35-49.

Nusem, E., Straker, K., & Wrigley, C. (2020). Design Innovation for Health and Medicine. Springer Nature.

Nusem, E., Wrigley, C., & Matthews, J. (2017). Developing design capability in nonprofit organizations. Design Issues, 33(1), 61-75.

Osborn, A. (1963) Applied Imagination: Principles and Procedures of Creative Thinking. New York: Scribner.

Osterwalder, A., & Pigneur, Y. (2010). Business Model Generation: A Handbook for Visionaries, Game Changers, and Challengers. Chichester/GB: John Wiley & Sons Ltd.

Osterwalder, A., Pigneur, Y., Bernarda, G., & Smith, A. (2014). Value proposition design: How to create products and services customers want. John Wiley & Sons.

Owen, S. (1979). The Use of Design Briefs in Local Planning. Department of Town and Country Planning, Gloucestershire Institute of Higher Education.

Papanek, V. (1971). Design for the Real World: Human Ecology and Social Change, New York, Pantheon Books.

Pickett, L. (2005). Optimising human capital: Measuring what really matters. Industrial and Commercial Training, 37(6), 299–303.

Pitt, J. (2008). Design Criteria in Architecture. In Vermaa, P., Kroes, P., Light, A & Moore, S. Philosophy and Design From Engineering to Architecture. Springer.

Plattner, H., Meinel, C., & Leifer, L. (2011). Design thinking. Understand – improve – apply. Heidelberg: Springer.

Quatman, G., & Dhar, R. (2003). The architect's guide to design–build services: John Wiley & Sons Inc.

Rampino, L. (2011). The innovation pyramid: A categorization of the innovation phenomenon in the product-design field. International Journal of Design, 5(1).

Rehman, F. U., & Yan, X. T. (2011). Application of context knowledge in supporting conceptual design decision-making. International Journal of Product Development, 13(1), 47-66.

Rittel, H., & Webber, M. (1973). Dilemmas in a general theory of planning. Policy Sciences, 4, 155-169.

Rowe, P. (1987). Design Thinking. Cambridge, Mass: MIT Press.

Rylander, A. (2009). Design thinking as knowledge work: Epistemological foundations and practical implications. Design Management Journal, 4(1), 7-19.

Rylander, A. (2009). Exploring Design Thinking as Pragmatist Inquiry. Paper presented at the 25th EGOS Colloquium, Barcelona, Spain, July, 2-44.

Sanders, E. B. N. (2002). From user-centered to participatory design approaches. In Design and the social sciences. CRC Press.

Sanders, L. (2008). An evolving map of design practice and design research. interactions, 15(6), 13-17.

Sarasvathy, S. D. (2001). Effectual reasoning in entrepreneurial decision making: existence and bounds. In Academy of management proceedings (Vol. 2001, No. 1, pp. D1-D6). Briarcliff Manor, NY. 10510: Academy of Management.

Schoemaker, P. J. (1992). How to link strategic vision to core capabilities. Sloan Management Review, 34, 67-67.

Schön, D. (1983). The Reflective Practitioner: How Professionals Think in Action. Ney York: Basic Books Publishing.

Senge, P. M. (2006). The fifth discipline: The art and practice of the learning organization. Crown Pub.

Sheen, R., & Gallo, A. (2013). HBR Guide to Building Your Business Case. Boston, Massachusetts: Harvard Business Review Press.

Simon, H. A. (2019). The sciences of the artificial. MIT press.

Sinek, S. (2009). Start with why: How great leaders inspire everyone to take action. Penguin.

Sternberg, R. J. (1999). Thinking styles. Cambridge University Press.

Straker, K., & Nusem, E. (2019). Designing value propositions: An exploration and extension of Sinek's 'Golden Circle' model. Journal of Design, Business & Society, 5(1), 59-76.

Straker, K., Mosely, G., & Wrigley, C. (2019). Identifying a set of line manager personas to guide new product introduction strategy. Strategy & Leadership, 47(4), 34-42.

Thompson, D., Tongo, M. and Chhabriya, M. (2012). The Role of 'Thinking Styles' and 'Creativity' in bringing about Organizational Change. International Journal of Scientific Research Publications 2(5), 1-5.

Turner, R. (2013). Design Leadership: Securing the Strategic Value of Design (1st ed.). London: Routledge.

UK Design Council. (2008). The Designing Demand Review. Available at: http://www.designcouncil.org.uk.

Ullman, D. (2009). Design: the evolution of information punctuated by decisions. DS 58-1: Proceedings of ICED 09, the 17th International Conference on Engineering Design, Vol. 1, Design Processes, Palo Alto, CA, USA, 181-192

Ullman, D. G., Dietterich, T. G., & Stauffer, L. A. (1988). A model of the mechanical design process based on empirical data. Ai Edam, 2(1), 33-52.

Van Boeijen, A., Daalhuizen, J., van der Schoor, R., & Zijlstra, J. (2014). Delft design guide: Design strategies and methods. BIS Publishers.

Varga, S. (2009). Brilliant Pitch: What to know, do and say to make the perfect pitch. Pearson Education.

Verganti, R. (2006). Innovating through design. Harvard Business Review, December, 1–9.

Verganti, R. (2008). Design, meanings and radical innovation: A meta-model and a research agenda. Journal of Product Innovation Management, 25(5), 436–456.

Verganti, R. (2009). Design-Driven Innovation: Changing the Rules of Competition by Radically Innovating what Things Mean. Boston: Harvard Business Press.

Wallace, G. W. (1995). Balancing Conflicting Stakeholder Requirements Balancing Conflicting Stakeholder Requirements. The Journal for Quality and Participation, 18(2), 84.

Wallas, G. (1926). The art of thought. New York: Harcourt, Brace, & World.

Walsh, V. (1996). Design, innovation and the boundaries of the firm. Research policy, 25(4), 509-529.

World Economic Forum, (2018. 10 skills you'll need to survive the rise of automation. Https://www.weforum.org/agenda/2018/07/the-skills-needed-to-survive-the-robot-invasion-of-the-workplace

Wright, P. M., & Mcmahan, G. C. (2011). Exploring human capital: Putting "human" back into strategic human resource management. Human Resource Management Journal, 21(2), 93–104.

Wrigley, C. (2016). Design innovation catalysts: Education and impact. She Ji: The Journal of Design, Economics, and Innovation, 2(2), 148-165.

Wrigley, C. (2017). Principles and practices of a design-led approach to innovation. International Journal of Design Creativity and Innovation, 5(3-4), 235-255.

Wrigley, C. & Straker, S. (2018). Affected: Emotionally engaging customers in the digital age. John Wiley & Sons Ltd.

Wrigley, C., Nusem, E., & Straker, K. (2020). Implementing Design Thinking: Understanding Organizational Conditions. California Management Review, 62(2), 125–143.

NOTES

DO!
SHINE A LIGHT ON ALL
ASPECTS OF A PROJECT

FIN!

DUUNNN DUNNN... DUUUUNNNN DUUN... DUUUNNNNNNNN
DUN DUN DUN DUN DUN DUN DUN DUN DUN DUN
DUNNNNNNNNNNN DUNNNN

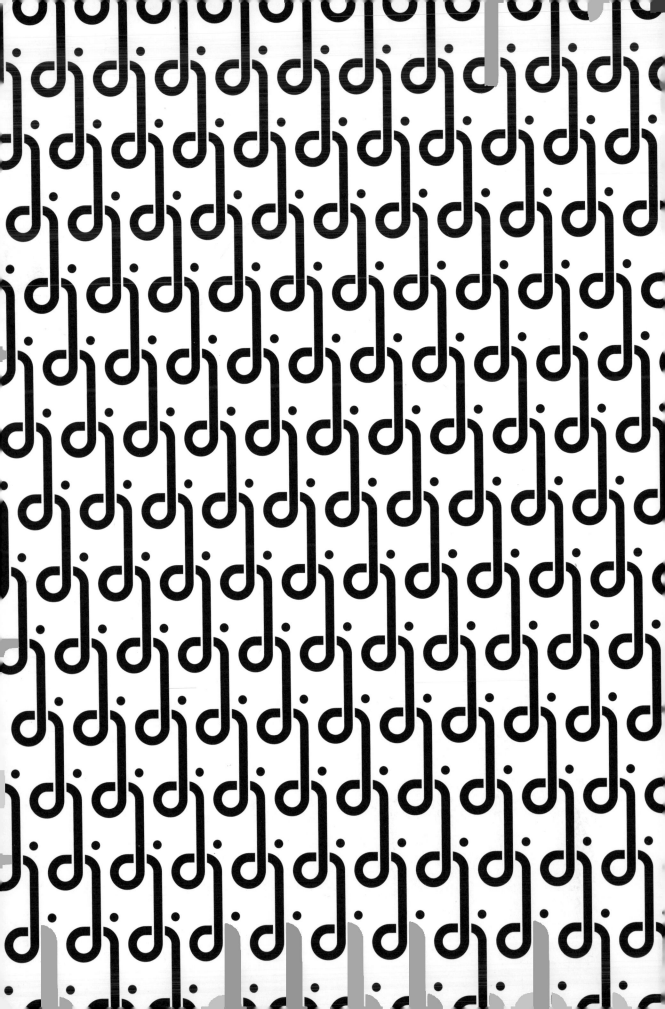